MEMOIRS OF
A MANGY LOVER

GROUCHO MARX

*M*emoirs of A

Illustrated by Leo Hershfield

MANGY LOVER

A Bernard Geis Associates Book

DA CAPO PRESS • NEW YORK

Library of Congress Cataloging in Publication Data

Marx, Groucho, 1891–1977.
    Memoirs of a mangy lover / Groucho Marx: illustrated by Leo
Hershfield.—1st Da Capo Press ed.
        p.   cm.
    "A Bernard Geis Associates book."
    Originally published: New York: B. Geis Associates, 1963.
    ISBN 0-306-80769-6 (alk. paper)
    1. Marx, Groucho, 1891–1977. 2. Comedians—United States
—Biography. I. Title.
PN2287.M53A3   1997
792.7′028′092—dc21
[B]   96-46945
                                                             CIP

First Da Capo Press edition 1997

This Da Capo Press paperback edition of *Memoirs of a Mangy Lover* is an
unabridged republication of the edition first published in New York in 1963.
It is reprinted by arrangement with Bernard Geis Associates.

Published by Da Capo Press, Inc.
A Subsidiary of Plenum Publishing Corporation
233 Spring Street, New York, N.Y. 10013

Books by Groucho Marx

BEDS
MANY HAPPY RETURNS
GROUCHO AND ME
THE GROUCHO LETTERS
DEAD SOULS
MARY POPPINS

This book was written in those long hours I spent waiting for my wife to get dressed to go out. And if she had never gotten dressed at all, this book would never have been written.

Foreword Is Forewarned

I know that the title of this book is misleading, but there's more than one way to sell a book or skin a cat. Actually there is no connection between these two statements, but I once had an aunt who kept saying that there was more than one way to skin a cat. One day, during a heat wave on the East Side of New York, she yielded to this impulse, and a few hours later a gent wearing a white coat came and carted her away. She was still holding the cat's skin. It wasn't a pretty sight. On the other hand, she was no bargain either.

Anyone buying this book is going to be out a tidy sum if he is sucked in by the title. I wish I could write a real sexy book that would be barred from the mails. Apparently nothing whets a reader's appetite for literature more than the news that the author has been thrown into a federal pokey for disturbing the libido of millions of Americans.

And now that the subject of sex has been disposed of, let's see what else there is.

Contents

Part One: L'Amour the Merrier

1 *Hurray for the Difference!*   3
2 *When Pigeons Fly In, Love Flies Out*   7
3 *A Blind Date Can Be a Pig in a Poke Bonnet*   13
4 *My Best Friend Is a Dog*   27
5 *Horsing Around with My Hormones*   33

Part Two: The Unnatural History of Love   39

Part Three: Social Notes from a Social
            Outcast

1 *Speed the Parting Guest*   69
2 *How I Beat the Social Game*   83
3 *The Pariah of Hollywood Am I*   91
4 *Adventures of an Extra Man*   97
5 *A Spirited Evening at Home*   103
6 *A Night on the Town, Medium Rare*   107

Part Four: It Happened to Eight Other Guys

1 *Scars Without Wounds*   115
2 *Calling with a Full House*   121
3 *Chico's Bank Account*   125
4 *A Hot Time in the Cold Town Tonight*   131
5 *Rats in the Cat House*   139
6 *The Prepaid Lover*   145
7 *La Leçon Française*   151
8 *One for and on the Road*   155

Part Five: Marxist Philosophy, According to Groucho

1 *What This Country Really Needs*   167
2 *On Thrift*   173
3 *On Luck*   183
4 *On Talent*   189
5 *On Polygamy (and How to Attain It)*   191
6 *On (and off) Bodies*   201

Epilogue: Off My Rocker   209

Part One

L'Amour
the
Merrier

1

Hurray for the Difference!

Until I was four I couldn't tell the difference between the sexes. I was going to say "the two sexes," but today there are so many variations that if one says "the two sexes" your friends are apt to regard you as a withered anachronism and wonder what rock you've been residing under for the past three decades.

My first realization that a fancier world existed dawned upon me one day when the only aunt I had who possessed both money and sophistication came to visit my mother. She was the wife of a successful vaudeville actor and, although still a young woman, had been to Chicago, St. Louis, and once had even spent the night in Denver. She had red hair, high heels, and a nice, tight shape that bulged where all desirable shapes were supposed to bulge. (I know that the word "shape" dates me, and I'm only sorry I wasn't old enough to date her.)

When she sailed into our flat, the whole area began to take on a tantalizing, exotic fragrance that later in life I recognized as the standard odor of a bordello. Of course at the time I had no idea what I was inhaling. For all I knew it might have been embalming fluid. But whatever it was, it was exciting, and certainly far removed from anything I had ever smelled before.

In our moth-eaten flat I was accustomed to the combined odors of four generally unwashed brothers, bean soup, and a kerosene stove that smoked. Now, here I was, breathing the heady perfume of the ages: a fragrance that made strong men tremble with desire and weak men whimper in despair.

My aunt was exceedingly pretty, and when she looked at me she smiled admiringly. Turning to my mother she said, "You know, Minnie, Julius has the loveliest big brown eyes I've seen."

Until that moment I had never given my eyes a thought. Oh, I knew I was nearsighted, but it never occurred to me that my eyes were anything out of the ordinary. Conscious now of my new-found charms, I lifted my eyebrows as high as I could and stared at her. She didn't look at me again but I continued to stare, hoping that if my eyes continued to bulge she would pay me another compliment. But no, she was busily gossiping with my mother and apparently had forgotten all about me. I kept walking up and down in front of her, hoping she would again say something flattering about my big brown eyes.

After some time my eyeballs began to ache from the unaccustomed strain, and her scent was making me dizzier and dizzier. I still couldn't seem to attract her attention, but desperate for another eulogy to my peepers, I began cough-

ing. Not a dainty little cough, but a steady, tuberculous, deep-throated blast, somewhat reminiscent of a Lesbian playing "Camille." As a result of this continuous coughing my head began to ache, but despite my constant attempts to squeeze another compliment out of her, she never noticed me again.

I finally realized that my case was hopeless and, reeling from my various ailments, I staggered from the room puzzled and feverish, but happy at the first compliment I had ever received from a woman . . . even if it was only a casual remark from an aunt.

It wasn't until much later that I looked into a mirror—and discovered that my eyes are gray.

2

When Pigeons Fly In, Love Flies Out

 Many years ago when I was young and single I was crazy about girls. This is not an unusual characteristic, especially in a young man whom destiny had marked as a potential sex maniac.

The truth is, if a young man doesn't like girls it is more than likely that eventually an analyst will tell him (I mean after four years at thirty-five dollars a throw) that he is either in love with his mother, his father, or the boy next door. I don't see how any part of this triangle could be much fun for a young man (or even an elderly one) and, besides, it is well known that sexual deviation is frowned upon by society at large. So my advice to all young men is to start chasing girls the day you start tying your own shoe laces, and forget all about the abnormal didoes that could eventually ruin you physically, morally, and, today, even politically.

Luckily, I was only interested in girls and myself, in that

order, and what was even luckier was that we were touring with a vaudeville act that was garnished with eight exceptionally good-looking babes. Since there were only four brothers, eight girls theoretically provided (if you're any good at mathematics) two girls for each brother.

There was only one girl I wanted, so this left seven girls for three brothers. When I say there was only one girl I wanted, I don't mean I wanted her permanently. All I wanted was to get her up to my room. She was a bonny lass (I was on a Scotch kick at the time) with red hair, a lovely body, and a perpetual smile that she generally turned on me.

One night after the last performance, we were sitting in the coffee shop of the hotel. I said, "Gloria," (as if this was a sudden thought, though actually I had been plotting it for weeks), "how would you like to come up to my room and split a bottle of champagne? It's domestic, but you can hardly tell the difference."

"Domestic champagne," she purred, "I love it. You won't believe this, but only yesterday I read an article in the Minneapolis *Tribune* by some vintage connoisseur in which he wrote that it is his firm belief that in many cases domestic champagne is superior to the imported stuff."

She still hadn't said that she would come up to my room, but her sudden enthusiasm for domestic champagne led me to believe that pretty soon her cute little body would be nestling in my bedroom.

I licked my chops in anticipation. Offhand, one would say that I had already won the battle. Unfortunately, this was far from the truth. The big trick was to maneuver her into my room. It was easy to get her past the desk clerk. The tough part was to outwit the hotel detectives. These hotel sneaks roamed the halls from sunset to sunrise, peering through keyholes and listening at cracks in the doors for sounds of hanky-panky. Theatrical troupes were always suspect, and if a hotel dick heard a female voice in a room that was supposed to be occupied by a single male, he would hammer on the door and shout, "If you know what's good for you, you'll get that woman outta there!"

I had a lovely room. It had a large bay window with double French doors. To allay suspicion, I had instructed Gloria to take the elevator to the ninth floor, where she roomed with another girl, and then walk up to the tenth. To cover my tracks, I took the back stairs and literally ran up the entire ten flights. The only thing that kept me going was the picture of Gloria, her red hair, and the kind of shape that, given a bit of leeway, could have made a shambles out of a monastery in five minutes flat.

I had given Gloria my extra key and eventually, with at least one palpitating heart, we met in my room. What a triumph! What vistas lay before me! I felt like Napoleon crossing the Alps or MacArthur walking on water!

It was a terribly hot night and, after securely locking and bolting the door, I flung open the French doors with a flourish that would have done credit to Rudolph Valentino, except that he always seemed to live in a tent with a sandy bottom. (I mean the tent's.)

Things were moving along nicely. The champagne tasted surprisingly good considering it was only two weeks old. As we sat there gazing hungrily into each others' eyes, a pair of pigeons flew into the room. It was rather a nice touch I thought. They were courting and we were courting. Except for the fact that I was wearing shoes and smoking a cigar, there wasn't a hell of a lot of difference between us.

As Gloria and I drew closer to each other, another pair of pigeons arrived. Then another pair. At first they nestled on the ledge of the bay window, billing and cooing. As an old bird lover I could tell by the sounds they made that their objectives were the same as mine.

After a while the ledge grew pretty crowded and a few of the more snobbish birds began to fly around the room looking for more restricted neighborhoods. As we all know, love-making can be a trying experience under the best of circumstances, but as the pigeon population increased, love-making was no longer practical. The entire bedroom became a dovecote and survival became the first order of the day.

I stopped talking to Gloria and began addressing myself to the birds, first in low, persuasive pigeon talk. This didn't help much so I then tried screaming. I guess they thought I was some kind of a nut who just hated pigeons, for they paid no heed to me at all and continued doing what comes naturally. I then realized that unless I could get these buzzards out of my love nest I was going to be out one quart of champagne and whatever else I had in mind.

I turned to Gloria. "Honey," I said, "would you mind stepping into the bathroom for a minute?"

She seemed surprised and resentful at this suggestion,

and rightly so. Our relationship had not yet arrived at the stage where one orders his loved one to go to the bathroom.

"Listen," she said, "I'm old enough to know when I have to go, and right now I don't have to go!"

"Unless you want me to get arrested," I pointed out, "you *do* have to go!"

"Now look here, you," she snapped, "just what do you have in mind that obliges me to go to the bathroom?"

Just then a pigeon flew past and nipped my ear lobe. I swung at it, but missed.

"Listen, darling, I love you," I said desperately, "but obviously we can't go on like this. The pigeons have taken over and I'm sending for the hotel detectives. I'm sure this isn't the first time pigeons have flown around this accursed bedroom, and I'm also sure the management has faced this problem before and knows how to handle it."

Gloria sniffed suspiciously, grabbed the bottle containing the remnants of the champagne and, with considerable dignity, wiggled her way into the bathroom.

Five minutes later I ushered two brawny flatfeet into the room. Without saying a word they took off their coats, closed the French doors, opened the hall door wide and started to flap their coats at the feathered interlopers. I watched them as they chased the pigeons down the hall. The detectives themselves looked like two large, evil birds of prey, pursuing their next meal.

I still don't know how they got the pigeons out of the hotel. Maybe they didn't. They may have chased them into the kitchen for next day's squab. All I was interested in was getting the birds and the detectives out of my room and Gloria out of the bathroom.

I again locked the front door and shouted, "Gloria, my sweet, I adore you! You can come out now!"

As she emerged she announced, "I feel sick and I'm going down to my room. This is the last time I'll ever touch domestic champagne!"

And that was the last time I ever got close to Gloria, except on the stage with seven other girls and three brothers. *Sic transit Gloria!*

3

A Blind Date Can Be a Pig in a Poke Bonnet

I was in New York, single, handsome, and dressed to kill, which is the last thing I was interested in. What I wanted and needed was someone to love, but I'd been away from Manhattan for some time and that little black address book I had cherished all those years was almost as empty as my head.

Hopefully, I thumbed through the wrinkled, yellowed pages and decided to call some of the old numbers. The first one I tried belonged to a cute little dish named Madeleine. I vaguely remembered her: nineteen, 36-24-36, and a complexion like peaches and cream. (Actually, I have no idea what kind of a complexion that is, but I've read this description in so many of Henry James's novels that I'm sure it must have something to do with the countryside in Surrey, and if it's good enough for good old Henry it's good enough for me.)

With beating heart I dialed expectantly, impatient to

hear the tinkling voice which, in other days, had always brought to mind the temple bells in Japan. (I must confess that the only reason I compared her voice to the temple bells in Japan is because I had just recently seen a rerun on the late late show of *Thirty Seconds Over Tokyo*. Well, let's forget about the war. It's an unpleasant subject and far too much has already been written about it.)

The number answered rather quickly, but what a letdown. These were no temple bells in old Japan! The voice that came over was a whiskey baritone of rare vintage. I don't know what he looked like, but in my mind's eye I visualized a stocky, broad-shouldered gorilla who probably drove a large meat truck for a packing company. At any rate, I was too frightened to ask where the fair Madeleine was. One thing I knew for sure—this was not Madeleine. And if it

were, I don't think I would have cared to spend the evening
with her.

I tried four more numbers. Two of the girls I called, sad
to say, weren't girls any more. It was strange, but they had
grown older, with husbands, children, kiddie cars, wet diapers, and rubber panties. (I don't mean the girls were wearing rubber panties, I was referring to the children.)

Now I was three down and two to go. The next girl I
called was named Prudence, and as I remembered her one
memorable night in a taxi, her name certainly belied her
behavior. Her mother answered the phone and babbled
away for fifteen minutes before I could even tell her my
name. She told me her daughter had gone into show business and was right now playing one-night stands with a
number three company of *Guy and Dolls*.

"You should see her," she said, "I caught her performance in Waterloo, Iowa, and even though I'm her mother
I must say she stood out like a sore thumb!"

This brief description of her daughter didn't sound too
alluring.

"Anyway," she rattled on, "if you want to get in touch
with her, I've memorized her route. From Waterloo they
were going to Dubuque, Cedar Rapids, Grand Forks, Fargo,
Upper Sandusky, East Liverpool, and then three days in San
Diego. They travel in style," she said proudly. "They've two
buses, one for the cast and one for the scenery. And remember that scene where the girls play Salvation Army lassies?
Well, they're supposed to be virgins, you know."

"Really?" I said, "I didn't know that—"

"Yes," she interrupted, "and there are twelve girls in that
scene but my daughter, Prudence, if I do say it myself, was
the only one who looked like a real virgin!"

I remembered Prudence that night in the taxi, and if she was a virgin, Joan of Arc played second base for the Cleveland Indians. As the old girl continued to sound off, I quietly hung up.

I then tried Celia, the remaining number in my little black book. I now had a total of fifty cents invested in phone calls. I remembered Celia very well. She was tiny, with contact lenses, a flat bottom and enough bust for all practical purposes. She was pretty, but, unfortunately, an intellectual. She lived in Greenwich Village and never went anywhere, even to the bathroom, without a thin, leather-bound volume of Emily Dickinson tucked under her arm.

I wasn't too crazy about this last call, but if you've ever been alone in a hotel room, a cold, drizzling rain beating against the window pane, and outside, the blowing of taxi horns reminding you of happy couples speeding to their various assignations, you know it wouldn't take much urging to persuade you to leap off the top of the Chrysler Building, let alone into the arms of Celia.

This last phone call just fizzled out like a wet firecracker. Celia apparently wasn't home, and if she was, she was probably doing something that's no good if it's interrupted.

Desperate and lonely, I decided to dine at the Colony. I quickly got dressed and, in my haste, stepped on my glasses. Luckily, I had my dark glasses with me and, though I could hardly see, apparently they recognized me for the maître d' quickly seated me at a table right near the kitchen.

As in all good restaurants, the service at the Colony is slow and leisurely, and by the time the consommé arrived I had read the menu forty-six times. I can still repeat it from memory, word for word, especially the prices. (Filet of sole with cream sauce . . . $4.25. Indeed! I can buy a whole bowl of goldfish and a year's supply of food for $1.75.)

Bored, I never realized what dull company I was until I sat there alone. I had heard everything I had to say time and time again, and I was in no mood to listen to me again.

All through the fish course, to distract my mind from the prices, I tried flirting with an attractive girl seated about eight tables away. I stared at her with my various expressions: sardonic, wholesome, debonair, wistful. Right in the middle of my wistful smile a small fishbone got stuck in my throat and the following five minutes were spent being thumped on the back by a bus boy, until nature finally relented and allowed the bone to slip down my craw.

"Enough of this meal," I said. "Bring me the check." As I started to leave I decided to have another look at the lovely creature who had almost caused my early demise. I casually sauntered past her table and, to my chagrin, realized that all my smiles had been in vain. The object of my affection turned out to be an elderly lady with a heavy Spanish mustache. I guess one should never wear dark glasses when flirting.

Despite a liberal potion of sodium amytal I slept fitfully all night. I dreamt not of marble halls, but of a girl in a number three company of *Guys and Dolls,* reading Emily Dickinson to a bus boy at the Colony Restaurant, while an elderly lady with a dark mustache danced in the Greenwich Village streets with a beefy truck driver named Madeleine.

The next morning fate came to my rescue. An ex-actor, who had been a monumental failure in the theater, read in some society column that I was in town and called to welcome me to New York, adding quickly that he was now a phenomenal success in the garment industry, and was there anything he could do for me?

These were the sweetest words this side of Paradise. I hadn't seen this chap in years but, as I remembered him, he knew a girl when he saw one. And now that he was a dress manufacturer I was sure he knew most of the desirable models in New York. Was there anything he could do for me? What a magnificent question! His words will live in my memory forever.

He asked me what I was doing in the big city and I truthfully answered, "Nothing." Oh, I was eating and sleeping, but I hadn't come to New York to sleep. At least not alone. I could do that in Chillicothe, Ohio, and probably better. What I was looking for was a companion—a dazzling, pulchritudinous wench who would hang on my every word and eventually obey my every command.

He didn't understand these words but his instincts were sure. "In other words," he said, "you want a dame."

"I sho' do!" (I said "sho'" deliberately to indicate the kind of Southern hospitality I was prepared to offer.)

My friend said, "Doll face" (this kind of talk is standard in the garment industry), "I got something for you like you've never seen before! She's a knockout! A one hundred per cent beauty! Of course she ain't too bright, but if you're looking for conversation I could line you up with a professor of English literature from Columbia. A very nice man of around fifty."

"Listen, jerk," I said, "junk the heavyhanded sarcasm and the preliminaries and get to the point. Just how and where do I meet this paragon of loveliness?"

"Well, she's working all day. Suppose you pick her up in the lobby of the Plaza at seven this evening?"

"That'll be just great!" I said, "but isn't it possible that there will be other girls in the lobby? How will I know her? Will she have a rose stuck in her ear?"

"Groucho," he laughed, "don't worry. You'll know her! She'll only be the most gorgeous girl in the lobby!"

Well, that was good enough for me. After breakfast I went out and had my glasses repaired. After lunch I had a massage, shave, haircut, manicure, and an hour under a sun lamp. I had been warned not to stay under it for more than fifteen minutes, but I wanted to be sure I looked athletic so I foolishly remained under the lamp for an hour. When they dragged me out, I fainted.

I called up a ticket broker and ordered two seats for *Death of a Salesman*—front row. I had never seen the play. I knew it wasn't a very happy one, but my father had been an unsuccessful salesman and I was curious to see whether this stage character was as unlucky as my old man.

When I arrived at the Plaza, having no means of identification, I decided I had better be careful whom I accosted. I saw many pretty girls flitting in and out the doors but most of them, sad to say, had escorts. I looked up toward the mezzanine and suddenly spotted an exquisite creature waving frantically and motioning for me to come upstairs.

As I approached I saw that she was accompanied by a short, well-dressed young man in extremely tight trousers, wearing considerably more jewelry than the average woman. It's difficult for me to describe her outfit, for I'm not very good at this sort of thing. She was wearing a gold lamé dress, golden sandals sans stockings, bright-red toe-nail polish, and her flaming red hair was topped off with a web of golden wires as high as an elephant's eye. I thought to myself, "If this aerial is electrically equipped, I can easily pick up Moscow and tell Khrushchev what I think of him."

Having surveyed her carefully I was now beginning to grow a bit uneasy about this pot-luck adventure. Moreover, I was puzzled by the peculiar little companion prancing at

her side. Conjecture took over. Just who was this elf? Was it her father? Her mother? Her brother? Her lover? While I was pondering this, she solved my problem.

"I'd like you to meet Cecil de Vere, my dancing partner," she said.

I bowed graciously. Now what? Were the three of us going to spend the entire evening together? "Dancing partner?" I echoed. She noticed the pained expression on my face. "Pardon me," I said, "but aren't you the model that Sam Bernie told me I was going to take out this evening?"

She giggled, gave her companion a playful shove and quickly explained, "Cecil and me were dancing this afternoon in a contest at El Morocco. We won first prize! A magnum of champagne!"

This sounded pretty good. Champagne for everybody. "Where is it?" I asked.

"Oh," she laughed, "I sold it to the bell captain. I usually meet him here on the mezzanine. We always split the money, and that's it. We sell every prize we win. Last week we won a Yorkshire terrier doing the Twist."

"Now wait a minute," I said, "you mean the dog was doing the Twist?"

"No, silly," she yelped, giving me a shove so vigorous that I damned near flew off the balcony. "*We* were doing the Twist. You know a dog can't do the Twist."

"Forget it," I said. "Get rid of tight pants," I whispered in an aside, "and we'll go to dinner."

"Cecil," she turned to him, "I'll see you tomorrow at El Morocco. Ta-ta."

He bowed slightly, extended a limp hand and scampered away.

"You know we're going to the theater," I told her. "Do

you have any particular place you'd like to dine?"

"Honey," she smiled, "I'm in your hands."

I thought to myself, "Not now, but perhaps later." I laughed so heartily at this silent sally that my glasses almost fell off again.

Outside, I hailed a cab. "Take us to Moore's Chop House."

Moore's is a famous restaurant in the heart of the theatrical district, and I had chosen it because I knew that from there we could get to the theater in a few minutes. What I had forgotten was that Moore's is probably the most brilliantly lit restaurant in New York. My companion was an extremely tall girl, and topped with that golden antenna she seemed about six-feet-one.

I am five-foot-seven-and-a-half, and we must have made a bizarre-looking couple as we walked to our table—talk about being the cynosure of all eyes! As we entered a hush fell over the restaurant. People stopped eating and drinking and just stared at this unbelievable-looking duo.

I had forgotten how loud she looked. Her outfit would have been sensational in a big musical revue, but in a brightly lit chop house frequented by bookies, gamblers, and show people, she seemed a little out of place. I began to wish I could slide under the table and have my dinner there.

We ordered drinks and I decided to engage her in conversation. At least that way I might be able to forget what I was looking at.

"Have you ever been to the Polo Grounds?" I ventured.

"No," she shook her antenna, she had no interest in polo. It seems she used to go with a fellow who played against the British polo team in Meadowbrook, Long Island, but they had had a falling-out because he spent almost all of his time with his horses. "I warned him," she said. "I told him one day, Foxhall, if you would rather be with a stinking horse than with me, you can go straight to hell! I guess this must have hurt his feelings because I never heard from him again."

"He probably took your advice," I said, "and is down there now." At the moment I wished I was down there with him.

In small words I tried to explain that they played baseball at the Polo Grounds, but she said she had never been to a ball game and has always been under the impression that baseball was stupid.

I then tried another track. "Where do you live?"

"Seattle," she said.

"That's quite a long way, isn't it?"

"Oh, no," she said quickly, "I go home every week end."

"Isn't that rather expensive on a model's salary?"

"Not for me," she smiled, "I have a friend in Seattle and he pays my plane fare."

Now I was sure that Sam Bernie was playing some kind of a vulgar joke on me. Who commuted weekly to Seattle?

Luckily, just then the food arrived and that ended the conversation.

As we stood up to leave, the restaurant grew quiet again. As before, everyone turned to stare as they watched this giantess and her tiny companion exit. For a moment I was afraid they were going to applaud.

We entered the theater about five minutes before the curtain rose. As we sailed down the aisle to the front row a hush came over the audience. Women stopped dropping their gloves, their escorts stopped picking them up, and all eyes were fastened on this mismatched couple as they went to their seats. I'm sure at no time during the performance would there be more eyes focused on the stage than were now looking at us. She looked like a sailboat with all its rigging up, riding high before the wind, and behind her trotted a sheepish nonentity, head bowed, trying desperately not to step on her dress.

Because of the headdress, she seemed even taller when she sat down than when she was standing, and I was positive that no one in the five rows behind her was going to see very much of the play.

For those who have never seen *Death of a Salesman,* it is one of the most tragic plays of our time. It's the story of a lonely, old, unsuccessful salesman who has been crushed by life and circumstances and whose emotions are torn between self-destruction and murder.

As the plot unfolded, the mood of the audience changed. The customary gaiety and babble that precedes a first-act curtain was gone. All was silent and tense.

Suddenly, to my horror, this empty, beautiful carcass sitting beside me burst out with a loud laugh that centered the attention of the entire audience upon her. I tried to sink lower in my seat but I was half-way to the floor as it was. Another six inches and I would have been in the orchestra pit.

I dug my elbow into her ribs. "Dear," I muttered with all the venom I could muster, "do be quiet. This is a tragic play and your laughter is annoying the audience."

"Tragic!" she yelped in a loud voice, "this is one of the funniest plays I've ever seen!"

"Well, it may be funny to you," I whispered, "but you're disturbing everyone else in the theater."

She broke into a hearty guffaw. "Groucho, you're always

kidding. You may think I'm dumb, but I know a funny show when I see one."

I suppose I could have sneaked out and left her there, but I was stuck with this lunatic and, since I had brought her there, it was my responsibility to the rest of the audience to get her out.

"Honey," I said, "I don't feel well. I'm sick to my stomach and I'm afraid I'm going to throw up. I've never thrown up in a theater before, and since this looks like a brand-new carpet I'd better get out on the sidewalk."

At this point the head usher came running down the aisle, recognized me and said, "Mr. Marx, is there something troubling your girl friend? She seems to be hysterical.

If you like, we can take her to the office and I'll call a doctor."

"Oh, no, this is nothing serious," I assured him. "It's rather intimate, but since you're the head usher I suppose I can confide in you. You see, her bra is too tight and it's pressing against her sciatica. Every time it does this it makes her scream and it sounds like laughter."

"Well," he said, "the management sent me down to tell you she's disturbing the audience."

I then grabbed her by the arm and said, "I'm sick. Come, let's go. I'll take you to the theater another night."

Reluctantly she left her seat and I literally dragged her up the aisle.

I'm sure that when Columbus first set eyes on America he was no happier than I was when, on exiting from the theater, I saw an empty cab standing at the curb.

"Eureka!" I shouted.

"What do you mean, Eureka?" she wanted to know.

"Nothing," I snapped. "That's the cab driver's name. Moe Eureka. I've had him before."

With that I opened the door and shoved her in, the golden aerial now slightly askew from the low entrance. I slammed the door, gave the driver ten dollars and said, "Eureka, take the young lady wherever she wants to go."

That empty hotel room didn't seem so uninviting after all. I blew a kiss at the rapidly disappearing cab and hurried down the street in the opposite direction, off into limbo.

4

My Best Friend Is a Dog

A man in my position (horizontal at the moment) is likely to hear strange stories about himself. For example, it was rumored a few years ago that I made a pig of myself drinking champagne out of Sophia Loren's slipper. This is sheer, slanderous nonsense. I am willing to concede that I tried to drink the bubbly stuff out of her slipper but she wouldn't take the damn shoe off her foot. So, while she wasn't looking, I drank it out of her handbag and nearly choked to death when I accidentally swallowed her lipstick along with the wine.

And now they say I am not a dog lover. Not a dog lover, indeed! Why, if I have a friend in the world it's my Great Dane bitch, Zsa-Zsa. We have been absolutely inseparable for years. The only reason she didn't come with me when I went to New York recently was that she didn't have the bus fare. Meanwhile, New York is a very lonely place without my dog. Actually, it's so lonely that when I see a

27

pretty girl with a dog in the hotel lobby, tears come into my eyes and I invite the hound into the bar for a drink.

In the eight years we've been together, Zsa-Zsa and I have never quarreled. Oh, occasionally she bites me but when she does I bite her right back. I'll teach her who's head of the house!

I don't spend any more on Zsa-Zsa's wardrobe than I have ever spent on any other girl, but she has never once asked me for a new collar just because the dog across the alley has a new collar. She has never sat in a night club with me and whined that Fred Astaire does the Twist and he's no kid so why can't I get off my butt and shake those old bones?

I give you my word that Zsa-Zsa has never said, "Dear, why don't you take a few dancing lessons? Really, nobody does the Bunny Hug any more."

Don't get me wrong. I am not suggesting that dogs will ever replace the fairest sex that blossoms in this great country of ours. That is something that every man will have to decide for himself. Personally, I don't see why a man can't have a dog *and* a girl. But if you can afford only one, get a dog. For example, if your dog sees you playing with another dog, does he rush to his lawyer and bark that your marriage is on the rocks and that he wants 600 bones a month alimony, the good car, and the little forty-thousand-dollar home that still has a nineteen-thousand-dollar mortgage on it?

Only once has a dog disappointed me. That was the time I took Alonzo, a big Saint Bernard, home from the studio. He had been working in a picture, earning twelve dollars a day, and he seemed lonely. I would have been even happier to take home a dog who earned fifteen hundred bucks a week. Lassie, for instance. But those dogs go with a much classier set than the crowd I hang around with.

At any rate, Alonzo was a very intelligent beast and his habit of running off with our brandy was, I suppose, typical of Saint Bernards, although many of my two-footed friends have done the same thing.

I was a little annoyed when Alonzo refused to eat the grub at my house. He said he preferred to take his meals at a nearby delicatessen. (Not that the food at my house isn't any good; I don't want people to get that idea, even though many of them have pointed it out to me. One woman said, "Your food isn't fit for a dog." Alonzo happened to be present that night and I think that's why he decided to eat out.)

Naturally my feelings were hurt when Alonzo walked out, but I kept my trap shut. After all, he was earning twelve dollars a day, which was eight dollars more than I was making at the time.

After he had been with me a week, I got the shock of my life. On Saturday night, just as I got through marking the liquor level on my brandy bottles, a little man stuck his head out of Alonzo's skin and asked for his salary—twelve dollars a day! Of course I should have suspected something was wrong the day my girl friend came into the living room with the cat. Instead of chasing the cat, as a dog should, Alonzo chased my girl.

Possibly it was this incident which gave rise to the ugly rumor that I am not a dog lover. People stopped inviting me to their homes—the same people who hadn't been inviting me for years. Ladies walked by without troubling to curtsy, and even my barber cut me. That hurt most. Nevertheless, to me it was enough that my dog kept his faith in me.

My overwhelming affection for dogs does not mean, of course, that I have no love for other pets. All my life I have had animals of one kind or another around the house, even if it was only a small distant relative or a skunk. (And believe me, there's not a great deal of difference.)

Once, when I was a child, I was given a pair of guinea pigs which, with a little difficulty, I learned to love like brothers. Incidentally, learning to love my brothers was much more difficult. Well, the two guinea pigs settled down in our cellar and one afternoon I discovered the cellar floor literally covered with the little creatures.

In those days my heart was smaller than it is now and I was able to love, at most, no more than thirty or forty guinea pigs. I was in a quandary. Did you ever spend an afternoon in a quandary with ninety-six guinea pigs?

"Sell them," my brother Harpo suggested.

"If that," I replied, "is all you have to say, you ought never to bother to speak again."

To this day Harpo has remained silent, and I can't tell you how pleased I've been.

Another brother, Gummo, came down to the cellar and he, too, said, "Sell them."

Since none of my brothers had any enthusiasm for these furry rodents, I took the hint and went to a near-by pet shop where I offered to sell my ninety-six guinea pigs for a paltry twenty dollars.

The dealer scratched his head. He then paced up and down the shop, kicking two guinea pigs who happened to be in his path. "Tell you what I'll do," he said. "I'll give you a hundred guinea pigs for nothing, throw in a cockatoo, and pay you three dollars in cash."

But let's get to the point of this story. For a good year-round pet, there is nothing to compare with a simple, un-pedigreed chorus girl. Like the Maltese cat, the chorus girl becomes attached to any man who feeds her. But, unfortunately, there the resemblance ends, for whereas you can take a Maltese cat to the basement for a saucer of milk the chorus girl insists on eating at the Pavillon or "21" where two people can get a good meal for around sixty-eight dollars. That is, if you don't tip the waiter.

A poor man's pet is definitely not a chorus girl, but nevertheless some day I hope to own one.

5

Horsing Around with My Hormones

Styles in medicine change almost as often as women's clothes. The health panacea of today becomes the deadly nightshade of tomorrow. Most of the coronary experts are now frightening their patients with the terrors of cholesterol. Today's fat man is torn between gluttony and survival. He is warned that if he does not shed his excess blubber he is halfway to the mortuary.

The foods that are recommended today are as palatable as a steady diet of wet blotters. Eggs are poison, and rich people who used to sneer at margarine are now lapping it up as though it were worth eating.

Last night I had a typical cholesterol-free dinner: baked squash, skimmed milk, and gelatin. I'm sure this will not make me live any longer, but I know it's going to seem longer.

I remember when every kid had his tonsils clipped, if his

parents had money. I knew one boy who had fallen arches. His mother took him to the doctor. That eminent physician, having no cure for fallen arches but desperately in need of some extra money for another year at medical school, removed his tonsils. The mother was so grateful for the removal of her son's tonsils that, as an added attraction, she allowed him to take out her appendix. Some months later he took her out. She even paid for that, but that's another story.

Several years ago, testosterone hit the front pages. This was a magic serum from Vienna which had been extracted from some part of a horse. Which part, I do not care to discuss publicly, but I'll tell you this—if it wasn't for that part, there wouldn't be any young horses today.

The theory was that if you took twelve shots over a period of three months, you would once again regain the vigor and vitality of a four-year-old stallion. For a man with low blood pressure and occasional suicidal tendencies, this seemed like a short cut to the legendary fountain of youth and all that it implied. An hour after reading this glowing article, I was in the doctor's office getting my first injection. Each morning on arising I looked hopefully in the mirror for my vanished youth. I saw many things in that glass. I saw a decrepit face bordering on degeneracy, a sagging chin, and enough decay to fill fifteen or twenty teeth, but nowhere did I see anything that resembled what I had hoped for.

After the twelfth stab with the doctor's magic bullet I came to the reluctant conclusion that this, too, was a snare and a delusion, that the doctor was a dirty crook and that the happy vista I visualized was a sexual mirage that could never be reached unless there was something to this nonsense about reincarnation.

Some months later, while on my way to the poorhouse, I ran into this charlatan (who was on his way to the bank) and who, by that time, had extracted two hundred and forty hard dollars from my pants and tucked them into his.

"Groucho!" he exclaimed, stepping back a few feet to survey me. "No, it can't be Groucho! Are you the same man

who came to see me three months ago, a total wreck? Why you don't look a day over thirty! Are you sure you're not Tony Curtis?"

"Of course I'm sure," I snapped. "I'm Groucho Marx and if you're still not convinced, I'll drive home and get my driver's license and show it to you."

He smiled falsely, but doggedly continued, "I presume the testosterone shots were effective, otherwise you would have been back to visit me. You look like a new man. How do you feel?" he asked, stroking the pocket with my money in it.

"I feel lousy," I answered.

"Hmmmm," he mumbled as he pulled his left ear lobe reflectively. "Are you telling me that the injections didn't work?"

"Oh, the injections worked fine, Doc, but the medicine wasn't worth a damn."

"Come now," he insisted, "didn't the testosterone do anything for you at all?"

"Well, yes it did," I admitted. "Yesterday I was out at Santa Anita and I did the mile in two minutes and ten seconds!"

Part Two

The
Unnatural History
of Love

Without assistance no man could write so monumental a chapter as this outline of love. Much valuable help was given to me by Dean William Emmish, Proctor of Lawford University, and by the Hon. William Doubloon, the Proctor of Procter and Gamble, makers of excellent soap—and let's keep this thing clean.

The writer would positively be a skunk if he didn't acknowledge his debt to *The Life and Loves of Colonel Harpo Marx,* by the Colonel himself, the underwear ads of the J. C. Penney Company, and Miss Phyllis Wiekowski, the chambermaid at the Mansion House in Jacksonville, Florida.

I must thank, also, the editors of the Encyclopaedia Britannica for their admirable volume, *Remo to Sog,* the publisher of *La Vie Parisienne,* that dandy little nudists' colony in New Hampshire, and the subscription salesman for *Life* magazine (for without his persistence I should never have bought the encyclopedia).

My thanks, too, to H. G. Wells's *Outline of History* and the monthly statement from Merrill Lynch, Pierce, Fenner and Smith. But my main source of information came from the filthy postcards I picked up on the side streets of Paris. And now, to begin.

Millions of years ago, love ran wild on this daffy globe of ours. Men were slimy creatures resembling a louse or the fellow your wife almost married. They were called amoeba —until they got money and changed their name to The First National Bank.

To be frank (and don't think I won't be), there was nothing lovable about the early amoeba. They had no small talk; their figures were certainly less attractive than those of any self-respecting financial statement, and they were flat broke. In fact, they lacked even spines, arms, legs, teeth, and eyes. But they had love.

It was, of course, fortunate that the amoeba couldn't see, because if he had been able to take one look at his mate the affair would have gone down the drain and our earth would now be as empty as the head of the average teenager. This is not to suggest that the amoeba was thinking of the future. His little mind was on nothing but his mate, whom he would meet under a stone and * * * * *

You know what the asterisks mean as well as I do, so don't get coy with me. If you'd stop leering for a moment and remember that this is a scientific treatise, we could cut the reading time of this trash from twelve minutes to nine and three-fifths, which is the same as the 100-yard dash. (Incidentally, I never could understand why, when they run the 100-yard dash, they're so eager to get to the finish line. If they would just remain at the starting line they wouldn't wind up sweaty and fatigued at the other end. But then, so many things in life are like the 100-yard dash.)

But I digress. As I said, the earliest men and women used to meet under a stone, which undoubtedly explains why their era was known as the Stone Age. Now they have the whole thing on the rocks—usually with bourbon or Scotch.

We will not devote much space to the Amoebolithic Age, because the amoeba contributed almost nothing to the development of love—unless you want to consider that trivial song, "Amoeba Wrong, But I Think You're Wonderful."

It was not until the oyster, which came immediately after the amoeba and right before the soup, that a touch of refinement was given to the tender relationship between the sexes. The male oyster was born with an instinctive understanding of feminine nature. He knew that if you wanted to get anywhere with a lady oyster you had to bring her gifts. So he hit upon the idea of making pearl. This was not the only ingenious thing the oyster ever did, for even today oysters make excellent stew, cocktails, and soufflés.

But don't misunderstand me. The oyster of today is not the oyster of fifteen million years ago, unless by any chance you happen to eat at Joe's De Luxe Sea Food Grotto when he's short on ketchup. And then they only taste the same.

Although the early oyster (*Oysterolithic Man*) led a full life, and birth control was comparatively unknown, he died out thousands of years ago. Why? Because the foolish oyster, idling away in his oyster bed, was an easy prey for more powerful living things. He had no protecting shell or armor to defend himself from (to name only one foe) the salmon, which was hostile and very cunning. The salmon, as you know, hides in tin cans and comes out only on Sunday evenings when your relatives pop in unexpectedly for dinner. The canned salmon is, of course, notoriously undersexed, and yet it has managed to survive. It is found in all ages and all good delicatessens, and is very nice with tomatoes and chopped onions.

I must point out that anthropologists fail to tell us how the earliest man learned the facts of love. My own deductions are that the amoeba and the oyster got their knowledge, just as you did, from the stories of flowers and their pollen and an exhaustive study of the *Tropic of Cancer* and *The Carpetbaggers.*

At any rate, after the plant life came animal life, then the Mutual Life, then the New York Life, and then the agent, telephoning you that your insurance had expired and so would you unless your next payment was received first thing in the morning. (This is known as a lapse. There are twenty-eight to a mile, and none of them is worth sitting on.)

We now leave the Oysterolithic Age, and no one is happier about it than I am.

Fifty-two thousand years went by—a mere flash in that unfathomable thing called eternity. Eternity! Its vast endlessness is difficult for the imagination to comprehend, but I think I can elucidate. Take, for example, the distance between the sun and the earth. Or, better still, take any number from one to ten. Double it. Add twelve. Subtract your original number. Is the answer nine? Of course it is!

Now, if you multiply that nine by millions of light years,

you get some conception of how important love later became to the hairy brute (*Homo Cavus*) sitting on a mossy rock outside his cave, wondering if the Dow Jones averages would ever go back up to where they were a few months ago.

Man had now acquired arms, legs, spines, and eyes. His chin had begun to recede along with his hairline, but a beard covered his face and he was now ready to apply for membership in the Union League Club. (Although the club had not yet even been conceived of, there were already members sitting in the windows—no doubt waiting for the building to be put up.)

In spite of his beard, the early cave man had the mentality of a child and it was only by instinct, rather than reason, that he could detect one sex from the other. He could tell a woman from a man, but he couldn't tell why. This primi-

tive ignorance was very embarrassing to the *Homo Cavus* until one rather advanced brute—Emig Bik—made a discovery. As he stood in front of his cave all day long, watching people come and go, the explanation dawned on him. The ones wearing skirts were women; the ones wearing pants were men—except in Scotland.

From that time on, life was considerably simpler. The cave man stopped walking on all fours because the same Emig Bik pointed out that if you walked on your feet you needed only one pair of sneakers instead of two. Thus the primitive genius who discovered women also invented economy—a logical and necessary sequence in those far-off times, as it is today.

Life was simpler, yet it still remained confusing, hazardous, and disturbing. All the elements of nature terrified the cave man. He shook with fear at the sight of lightning, and when thunder roared he blamed it on the gods and wished that he could invent writing so he could write a letter to Dear Abby.

The early cave man (*Porgie Amok*) was sullen and fearful on stormy days. When it rained he remained in his cave instead of going out to kill bears, deer, and dinosauri. To be sure, he was dressed to kill, but the winds howled and the rains poured and primitive man was afraid.

In his cave he found nothing but boredom. He had not yet learned to talk to his mate. And love—human love— was something he knew nothing about. (Children were not discovered until the following year.) So the cave man and his mate sulked and growled at one another while they waited for the rain to cease.

They waited one day, two days, three days, a week, but the storm's fury continued and, finally, there was no more food left in the cave. The primitive man was hungry and so was his wife, who said nothing—chiefly because language had not yet been invented.

The brute man glowered at his wife. If the rain didn't end pretty soon he would be compelled to munch on her—and she knew it. She grunted, which was her way of letting him know that she hoped he'd find something else to satisfy his hunger, but the rain went on and on.

The time had come. With a savage growl, Porgie Amok leaped for his wife and started to bite her shoulder. As he did this, his paw touched the woman's flesh. The touch of her gave him a strange, exhilarating sensation. He bit her again—this time more tenderly. His hands strayed through her tresses and his soul tingled. Then instinctively he threw his gnarled, ape-like arms around her soft white shoulders and felt his body pulsating against hers. She, too, felt and was astonished by this amazing new sensation. Their bosoms heaved; there was ecstasy in their embrace as they panted out what to you would be mere guttural grunts but what to these primitive people were the first sweet sounds of love. I could go on like this for pages and pages, eager reader, but I, too, am only flesh and blood, and I've got to keep my mind on my work.

Eventually the storm came to an end and the early brute man was sad. He didn't want to go out. While his neighbors were roaming the fields in search of food, he stood at the edge of his cave, hopefully peering at the skies for the first sign of rain. He wanted to tell his friends how the storm had brought love into his life, but, as I said, there was no common language. No language at all—only grunts which meant, "How are you?" "I'm fine, how are you?" "Can't complain." "Say, you look very well with the hair on your chest bobbed." "Glad to hear you say that. My wife thinks I look like a brontosaurus."

So, with silent eagerness, Porgie waited for rain. Love was just around the corner. One afternoon the clouds in the distance told him it was going to rain in the valley thirty miles away, and he started off in that direction as fast as his squat legs could carry him. In his wife's opinion he was going hunting and, in a way, she was right.

After running till nightfall Porgie reached the valley where, sure enough, it was raining. His heart sang as he entered a cave and found a woman alone. . . .

The discovery of love spread like wildfire. Porgie became known as The-Great-Lover-Who-Waited-For-Rain. He waited, too, for the invention of a language so he could tell the boys at the bowling alley about his amorous exploits. If there had been words he could have composed a little poem about himself:

> *Orgy Porgie,*
> *Pudding and pie,*
> *Kissed the girls*
> *And made 'em cry.*

But there were no words. And there was no rain!

Once it looked as though the skies were about to weep, and Porgie made love. And love made of Porgie a prophet once more. For it didn't rain, after all, and our *Homo Cavus* discovered that the mating season is not dependent upon inclement weather. The mating season opened (then, as now) on January 1 and ended on December 31.

A year passed. A little brute was now sitting in the corner of Porgie's cave, sharpening a rock on his feet. He was named Stone Face and the cave man and the cave woman grunted. In their simple way they were content. They didn't know that a new civilization was springing up in the Far North.

As for the *Glacial Age* (between forty-five and seventy among the Latin people), we need not concern ourselves about this period for long. It has been called an age of frigidity among the sexes, but this is probably an inaccuracy.

All in all, there was little to interest the *Glaciolithic Man*. Around him there was nothing but ice, which was obviously worthless without mineral water or ginger ale, and it was no common occurrence for him to return home in the evening and find his mate just as cold as the ice. Women, too, came home to find their husbands icy. The task of warming them up was a tedious one and far from proving an incentive to love.

Professor H. M. S. Wimpble tells us of a Glaciolithic woman who, on entering her igloo, found her mate frozen in the arms of another woman. After heating them back into consciousness, she said to her husband, "Who was that lady I thawed you with?"

Her husband's reply is not on record because Joe Miller had not yet been born. All in all, however, it was a most unpleasant age.

Many people write about love wtihout ever having come in contact with it. But until you have brushed a woman's cheek with your trembling lips and brushed your shoes with your wife's new guest towel, you know nothing about love —or your wife.

Love is not something you can learn from books, for

love is an elusive sprite that leaps from nook to cranny and taps you with its magic wand, then flits away like the first hounds of spring. (It's not such a bad piece of writing, that

last sentence. I've seen worse in books that sell for five dollars. In fact, that's where I saw this.)

But getting back to love (*Cardia Hortarium*), I want to assure my readers that this outline is the real McCoy—fearless, and no quarter asked or given. As I wrote to Professor H. M. Thorndyke of the Boston Anthropological and Wet Wash Society (who, now that I think of it, never answered my letter), I am willing to guarantee the truth of every word. If anyone can prove that there is a single inaccuracy in one of these pages, I will gladly donate five thousand dollars ($5,000) to the MRS. GROUCHO MARX FOUNDATION FOR THE CARE AND BETTERMENT OF MR. GROUCHO MARX and, as second prize, fifty cents (50¢) to each of the kids.

Be sure to write legibly on only one side of the paper, even if it's only a postcard saying it's been raining every day and that Aunt Molly has had another baby.

I'm not going to tell you much about the Dark Ages because we historians know very little about that period. Frankly, it was so dark that no one could see what was going on, and those who did see were too polite, or embarrassed, to tell.

At any rate, we know that plenty did go on in the Dark Ages. I know, for example, what used to happen in our house when the parlor was dark. My brother, Harpo, in looking for the piano, often would play the maid by mistake. It wasn't long before the neighbors complained. And the maid, too. For she, in her sweet, childlike way, happened to be in love with my father. It was a gentle, unspoiled, girlish devotion. All she asked was that he sell the children and run away with her to New Jersey, where her brother had a farm on which he raised little farmers and big welts on his wife's back. (This was before the agricultural schools introduced scientific irritation as a substitute for rain.)

To my father's everlasting credit, it must be said that he never for a moment thought seriously of selling the children and running away. "What would anyone give me for five used boys?" his voice boomed throughout the old broken-down mansion. "I think I'll stay right here."

That's the way Ole Marse Marx was, back there on the plantation. And that, no doubt, is why the slaves loved him for his kindness, his understanding, and for the fact that he was the only landowner in the county who had never owned a whip. (To show their gratitude, the slaves took up a collection and bought my father a whip, with which he laughingly used to flog the living daylights out of them.)

As I have tried to indicate, life in the Dark Ages was in a constant state of confusion. History tells us of a hungry Neanderthal man who, unable to see where he was, began eating the edge of his cave. He supposed it was spinach with perhaps a touch more than the usual amount of sand. Whereupon his wife said, "Remember, you can't have your cave and eat it too!" But the poor Neanderthal man, not knowing what she was talking about, continued munching until he had eaten them both out of house and home. That was how the expression was coined, for since they didn't have money in those days either, all they could coin was expressions.

Polyandry is the marriage of one woman to a group of men. Unheard of in the Stone Age and Iron Age, and only rumored about in the Dark Ages, polyandry made its first appearance in the Bag Age, those dismal years when a man couldn't take a woman to a hotel unless he had a suitcase or a woman. Anyway, there were no hotels at the time, thus making it possible for a traveling man to stop at farmhouses where there was only one bed and many fine jokes, which I won't bother to clean up here.

52 · *MEMOIRS OF A MANGY LOVER*

All this, as I say, happened in the Bag Age. Which reminds me that among the Romans women were called "baggage." Since then a girl has often been called a "pretty baggage." And Mrs. Gladstone, wife of the great English statesman, was known as the first Gladstone bag. What I'm trying to say is that polyandry splits up the alimony payments instead of placing the entire burden on one man—but then, money isn't everything!

Love was none too easy for the prehistoric man. It's no bargain now, either. The trouble with love is that many people confuse it with gastritis. After the ailment has been cured they find out they're married to a girl they wouldn't be caught dead with.

Some of the earliest by-products of man's love were the beauty parlor, bicarbonate of soda, and the family. The family, as you probably know, is a social unit based on the instinctive grouping of all animals—such as your wife's mother, your wife's two sisters (who probably never will get a man) and your wife's brother, who hasn't worked in eight years.

You will notice that the group contains none of your family, only hers. It was that way in the Dark Ages and it's that way now.

If you want to send ten dollars to your father you have to keep it quiet, or your wife will say you didn't marry your father—which is perfectly silly because your father is already married, and happy, too—providing you send him the ten dollars, which you probably won't—times being what they are and your father being what he is. I guess that takes care of the family. I only wish it took care of mine.

The cave man, having no language, could talk only with

his hands. When he wanted to tell his mate he loved her, he socked her on the chin. When he wanted to say, "I'm hungry," he socked her on the chin. Sometimes he socked her on the chin merely to see if she could take it, and all this was confusing to the silent little woman, for she seldom talked back. When she did, her husband would sock her on the chin again. This sort of conversation became known as "chinning." True, the little woman could say a few things in pantomime, but they were pretty dull, as they are to this day.

It was obvious that the world needed a language. And, as history has shown us, necessity is the mother of invention, just as the last one over the fence is a nanny goat. So, in a short time (a mere thousand years as the crow flies—or five hundred if it's an eagle), the first crude language was being heard. The words were few, but they were all that those primitive people really needed.

MAN'S FIRST VOCABULARY

Unga Unga	Ash Ash
Glub Glub	Throw me those water wings
OOscray Icquay	If I catch you fooling around my wife again I'll cut your heart out.
Deportment	A
ZUM Zum Zum	Dearie, your underskirt shows
Ugh	How's your wife?
Nugh	How do you suppose?
Mug	I was just being polite.
Lug	Mind your own business!
Rug	Royal Wilton, 20 x 14, $149.95
Bing	Crosby
John Cromwell	A friend of the family who has just returned from India.

The early brute-man now had a language, which did much to make those long winter evenings bearable. Remember, he couldn't take his woman to a theater or club. The best he could do was take a club to his woman, but that wasn't something that both of them could enjoy, so they stayed home and jabbered. The man could tell his mate how he slew a tiger with his bare hands and how the boss had said, "J.B., that was as fine a little job of tiger-slaying with bare hands as I've seen in months." And the little woman would say (there were times when the husband wished she hadn't learned to talk), "Well, then why doesn't he pay you more? Joe Grant hasn't killed a tiger all season and he gets twice as much as you do!"

"MMM-mmm-mmm," the man would purr as his warm lips smacked hers. Or maybe it was his fist. At any rate, winter soon passed and spring came. And oh, how good it was to be alive and young! The lovers could now play their games outdoors, and the games were many. But most of all they liked to play duck on the rock—when they could find a duck. The rocks, of course, were plentiful. In fact, rocks were an essential article in every home with children. Usually it was a well-aimed rock that put the infant to sleep, and the mother crooned "Rock-a-bye, baby," as the brat passed out cold.

Thus the Neorockolithic Age came to an end and a new world was born, a world infinitely more complex and less satisfactory. Where Stone Age man needed only a woman for company during those long nights in the cave, the new man (*Homo Sap*) cluttered up his life (and his cave) with real company. Society took the place of sex, and "party" came to mean dinner at eight instead of a frolic *à deux*.

Thus, the Age of Social Man took over, and real love flew out the window.

As we continue this study of The Unnatural History of Love, we get closer and closer to modern times. This creates the illusion that we may be getting to the point.

The reader must bear in mind, however, that history repeats itself—and don't think I won't before this is over. Well, history can take a back seat—and a good shot of bicarbonate of soda.

We now come to the Middle Ages, and I can assure you that you couldn't be any more surprised than I am. The Middle Ages was—were?—a period of slow progress. People just didn't care whether they invented anything or not. But that didn't affect love. It had already been invented. That is, the basic elements. The only thing left to do was to clear up certain moot points.

Many a night a crowd of minnesingers would gather around the great Yule log in the baronial hall and try to clear up some of these points, but what with the heat from the log and the heat from the grog, it wasn't very long before they were all plastered and forgot what they were there for. That was the trouble with the Middle Ages, no intestinal fortitude.*

We now come to the Renaissance, but don't ask me how. Actually, I meant to include this in a previous chapter but it took me all week to learn how to spell it. The Renaissance was not a political or religious movement. It was a state of mind. It's probably hard for you to believe that such a long word had nothing to do with love. That's pretty absurd

---

* No guts.

of you. Rheumatism is a fairly long word and yet it has nothing to do with love. But don't get the idea that rheumatically inclined people aren't susceptible to love. In many cases, that's how they got that way. The trouble is they just can't get around like the younger squirts, and when you're in love you've got to be able to cover a lot of territory. Fortunately, I have a two-seated Vespa.

Where were we now? Oh, yes. In the Renaissance people once more dared to be happy just because they were alive. They no longer concentrated all their thoughts upon the blessed existence that awaited them in Heaven. They tried to establish their paradise upon this planet and, truth to tell, they succeeded to a remarkable degree.

Love was going great guns. Women began to regain some of their freedom. No longer was it necessary for them to sneak around the corner for a Vodka martini. Openly and unashamedly, they began to assume their true role as man's

mate and companion. Woman was coming into her own. It was at this time that someone got the idea of yoking the women to the oxen. Historians are divided as to how this affected civilization. A few of them think this was a step backward, but most of them believe with me that it was definitely a step in the right direction. Whatever they think, it certainly was a big help to the oxen. The dumb brutes (the oxen) are grateful to this day. So grateful that whenever they see a woman they tip their horns*—unless they happen to be wearing a hat.

Possibly a cross section of the daily life of a typical Renaissance family will best show the advancement of love and sex at this time:

THE CHARACTERS:	Mr. Dinglefingle and Mrs. Dinglefingle
THE SCENE:	The parlor of their split-level hovel
THE TIME:	Ten o'clock at night
THE NIGHT:	Before Christmas

MR. DINGLEFINGLE IS SPEAKING.

MR. DINGLEFINGLE: You know, darling, love is the sweetest thing.
MRS. DINGLEFINGLE: And how!
Finis

This really isn't the finish, folks, but it's all we can print. As a matter of fact, it's only the beginning. Henry Miller, take it away!

These were, indeed, glamorous days. Love had forged

* Many cattle breeders declare that the ox is the horniest animal extant.

ahead so swiftly that in no time it had displaced agriculture as the leading industry of the period. To anyone who has tried both, this won't come as much of a surprise, and it didn't surprise either the peasants or the nobles. In fact, they caught on almost immediately. They were quick to see that agriculture was a seasonal occupation and a form of husbandry that could only be practiced successfully through the spring and summer. Love, on the other hand, knew no seasons. It could be pursued not only through the tepid and heated months, but even more successfully through the long frigid days (and nights) of winter. Besides, it was much easier on the back.* At any rate, it was much nicer to drop in on your lady friend than to drop seeds in the ground, except that occasionally your lady friend wasn't there and the ground always was.

Medieval authorities are now practically unanimous in saying that the sudden tremendous increase in population during this period was undoubtedly attributable to the revival of love. At this time, if it isn't too late, I personally want to thank the Renaissance women for the enthusiastic zeal with which they threw themselves into this movement. Women of this type don't exist any more.

Love was undoubtedly responsible for the increase in population, but even love (powerful as it is) requires the assistance of the sterner sex, and the sterner sex was busily occupied during this period, opening up new trade routes. What, then, was the answer? Could it be solved? It remained a mystery for centuries. It wasn't until last Friday, a year ago, that Dr. Max Krum, author of *Love and Trade Routes,* advanced a theory that was flouted and accepted in the same

* Oh, yeah?

breath. He said that a roving tribe of Goths descended upon the cities just as the husbands blew for the trade routes. They unstrapped their guitars and, strolling up and down the main streets, crooned, "I've Goth five dollars." It wasn't long before the girls were that way about the Goths and the Goths were this way about the girls.

The duennas, however, quickly saw that this exchange of currency was giving the towns a bad name and they issued a decree that forced the local ingenues to remain indoors. It was thus that the popular expression came about, "We can't ever duennathing."

As the population increased cities began to displace the feudal estates. This made it necessary to form a new system of government. The merchants banded together and wrote a charter which they thought fitted the needs of the municipality. They elected a Senate and a Duke (or Doge). When they elected a small man as Doge, they called him Gitalong Little Doge. They didn't call him that long, though, because the copyright owners, spending the summer in Antibes,* heard the phrase and started suit in the supreme court for damages amounting to 300,000 florin. It would be hard to say what a florin is worth in American money (it's even hard to say what a dollar is worth in American money) but, at any rate, the girls often woke up with 100,-000 florins under their pillows when a Goth had to leave town suddenly. So, the suit must have been for about six dollars in round numbers.

The Renaissance world ate a great deal of fish.† This will give you an idea of the type of people that existed in

---

* Fashionable watering resort.
† Before Cholesterol.

those days. If it does, send your idea to the editor and he will forward it to your reporter who can use all the help he gets. But to get back to this fish thing, it was just something else to keep the men away. It was always something. In the twelfth century it was the Crusades. In the thirteenth century it was the call of the sea and in the fourteenth it was fishing. The husbands spent seven months of the year fishing and seven months looking for worms. You'll probably say that this makes fourteen months. I expected it. Well, for your information, the year had fourteen months in those days. That'll teach you to keep your nose out of this. So you see, once again it was a pretty tough struggle for the housewives.

The stories that Marco Polo (discoverer of the North Polo and South Polo) told about his travels aroused no little interest in the strange lands beyond the confines of Europe. In spite of this interest, exploration proceeded very slowly because the sea was still unpopular. There were many good reasons for this. The boats were small and inadequate, hardly as large as our modern ferry boats. In one respect, however, they were better. They didn't have violin players on board, begging for nickels with one hand and playing "The Rosary" with the other.

The compass was still a new instrument and had not yet been perfected. In those days if you wanted to go north by northeast by east, you'd have to steer a course south by southwest. You can realize what a strain this was on the Renaissance mind. Naturally this led to a great deal of confusion, and it got so that people just didn't care where they landed; that is, unless they had a fight, and then they landed on each other. An explorer would start out to discover India or Arabia and end up four miles north of Sandy Hook with a bad cold. This was the beginning of pneumonia and the mustard plaster. From then on, all sailors wore rubbers unless they came home with a rolling gait.

Vasco da Gama, a first-rate explorer in his time, although today he'd probably be considered a bum, cursed the invention of the compass till the day he died. It seems that on one of his voyages he had planned to go to the tropics and outfitted his crew accordingly. After three days at Abercrombie & Fitch, they came out with white flannels, straw hats, sport shoes, a suitcase full of Bacardi, a little red book full of telephone numbers, and a bill for $609. After carefully maneuvering his ship with one eye on the compass and one eye on a chorus girl that luckily happened to be passing, he looked up and, much to his dismay, saw straight ahead of him the icy shores of Labrador. You can well imagine his embarrassment when he landed with a crew dressed for Florida weather. They're still laughing about it up in those parts. I think it's pretty funny myself, although not funny enough to laugh at.

About this time there was much speculation concerning the shape of the earth. Of course, dear reader, it's not my place to expound theories of my own, and I wouldn't want anything I tell you to get around, but there is no question in my mind but that the earth's a perfect triangle. And if it's proof you want, I have plenty. Why is it that all fish swim under water? Why is it that people go to Florida in the winter and Quebec in the summer, or vice-versa? Why is it that a person will never open third hand vulnerable unless he's got three and a half tricks? Just ask anybody who thinks the world is round these questions and see what he answers.

I don't expect you to catch the meaning of what I have just written until you have reread the above paragraph a number of times. Personally, I think you'd be a sucker if you did. I read it six times, myself, and I still don't understand it.

While we're fiddling around in the fifteenth century, it would be absurd to overlook one of the greatest discoveries of all time—America* the beautiful. The credit for this

* Longitude 8493, Address unknown.

must go to one Christopher Columbus, a Genoese sailor, whose firm convictions were that the earth was a sphere and that his only mission in life was to prove it to himself and the world. In despair, he solicited help from Spain and Portugal. Portugal didn't even answer his letter. It turned out later he was full of saltpeter at the time and, in his dazed condition, had neglected to enclose the letter and had just sent the envelope.

However, Queen Isabella of Spain, who was nuts about bearded sailors, agreed to supply him with three ships and eighty-eight men. This meant twenty-two quartets if they could all sing, or twenty-nine trios if they couldn't.

After a cold supper of curd and betel nuts, he set sail in the year 1497. All right, make it 1492. But not a year earlier!

Just after Columbus set sail from Spain, Queen Isabella heard some nasty gossip about him and began to entertain doubts as to what he was really after. It later developed that the real reason for his voyage was not to prove that the earth was round (that was only a gag; he knew it was square) but to see a dame in America whom he'd contacted through a "Lonely Hearts" column unbeknownst to Isabella. He'd been corresponding with her for years. They'd even swapped photos. He had sent her one of Valentino and she sent him one of Tuesday Weld. (She was no fool, either.) Now you're probably going to tell me that there was no transatlantic mail in those days. This is undoubtedly true, but it's also true that love always finds a way. What about Adam and Eve, for example? Or Frankie and Johnny?

When this scandal broke, Columbus, fortunately, was all at sea and far out in the ocean. His first stop was the Canary Islands, but he didn't tarry there very long because he discovered that all the people there were canaries and they kept flying into his beard. So it was Bye Bye Birdie, and away we go!

He sailed on for sixty-two days and sixty nights (he lost two nights in the Azores in a poker game), and finally one bright morning a member of the crew sighted a branch of berries floating nearby. This meant land (or a marine fruit store). When Columbus was notified of this he crawled out of a coal bin where he had been hiding from the crew and, pointing to the fruit, said, "Gentlemen, I think we've got something there."

When the sailors disembarked at San Salvador they were hungry for both food and women. Don't forget, this had been a long journey. It is true they hadn't seen food in thirty days, but they hadn't seen women in sixty, so you can well imagine what they went looking for first. You know how it is when you're on a transatlantic liner for five days and you don't meet anybody but three buyers with trench coats and trench mouth, and four school teachers who are seasick all the way over. Well, that will give you a fair idea of how the sailors felt when they trooped off that mud scow. History tells us that even the mermaids weren't safe. As for the Indian girls, it goes without saying—well, I guess I won't say it then. I'll tell you about it in the proper time and place. How about your house next Wednesday afternoon?

Now let us leave Columbus and his sex-crazed crew and jump back to Europe for a moment. I'll pay half the fare if you'll pay the other half.

Although most of Europe's attention was drawn to this new promised land that lay across the vast seas, we must not lose sight of the fact that great things were happening at home.

Italian cities were beginning to attain positions of importance. There was a definite historical reason for this, but in an outline of love you can't fool around with historical reasons, definite or otherwise. (And if I did happen to feel in the fooling-around mood, I'd be crazy if I picked a historical reason.)

Of these Italian cities, Venice was easily the most important. Some of you who have read Gibbon's *The History of the Decline and Fall of the Roman Empire* will probably say that Rome was the most important, but if this were so, why did they bury both Rome and Gibbon? You notice they didn't bury Venice. Anyway, don't keep asking so many questions. If you have no confidence in the writer, you may as well drop out right here. There are a lot of things I'd rather be doing than this. I could be out on the courts brushing up on my backhand if Hans, the lengthier of my two dachshunds, hadn't gnawed a hole in my tennis racket this morning. I'm sure that Spengler, Van Loon, or Alcott* would never have been what they are today if they had had to contend with silly questions and dachshunds that ate their tennis rackets. The same reader who was so quick to say that Rome was greater than Venice is the same type of flathead who said that the Dow Jones Averages would climb to a thousand. And now where is he? Or where are they for that matter?

But let's get back to Venice itself. As you doubtless know,

* Spengler—*The Decline of the West.*
Van Loon—*The Story of Mankind.*
Alcott—*Little Women* (RKO).

Venice was built on a mud bank. Don't ask how. It just was, that's all. I don't know anything about mud banks. I don't know anything about any other kind of banks, either, as I learned the hard way in 1929 when they folded up with my dough inside of them. All I know about mud banks is that in the early Venetian days mud was used for money, thus mud banks. Curiously enough, we still require mud banks, even in these modern times. When gold was discovered in the Far West, it was called "pay dirt." I'm sure you have all seen photographs of hardy miners dishing dirt.*

I know this sordid discussion of money hasn't much to do with sex, but just try to take a girl out, when you're broke and see how far you get. I tried it one night and was back in bed at eight o'clock—alone . . . with nothing to amuse me but a cold hot water bag.

* Louella Parsons and Hedda Hopper.

Part Three

Social Notes
from
a Social Outcast

1

Speed the Parting Guest

Seated at a stone table in a darkened cave and gnawing on a bone, sits our hero—that's me, Groucho Marx, the Hermit of Hollywood.

Good-by to Spode dishes, Amontillado sherry, and finger bowls; good-by to dinner at eight, dinner at seven, or dinner at all—I'm yesterday's host! As soon as my wounds heal, I'm coming out of my cave and resuming my social career, but not as a host—oh, no—that's the hard way! Let that certain restaurant be the nation's host from coast to coast, and let me be the nation's guest.

The guests are the white-haired boys and girls. The hosts are the chumps. I've thrown my last party and now, before I close my mouth and cave for the winter, I would like to set down a few warm memories of guests who have nibbled at my groaning board.

For those of my readers who have never seen a guest, they are easily described. They are either tall or short,

69

slightly run-down at the heels and come in all of the popular colors. A guest can be further identified as one who comes to your house by invitation. The one who comes without an invitation is either a black widow spider or a relative.

There are all kinds of guests. There is the dinner guest, the week-end visitor, the monthly guest, and, if you're not careful, the permanent guest. But the most innocent, friendly, and comparatively harmless of all these is the dinner guest.

A dinner party is usually composed of a group of six, eight, or ten people. The size of the party, of course, depends a good deal on the size of the dining room and, in many cases, on the size of the cook.

A word about cooks: most cooks are either just getting married or just getting divorced, and it is wise to plan your dinner parties with this in mind. Obviously, you are apt to get a much more satisfactory dinner while the cook is courting than you are while she is going through the cooling-off stages with her current incumbent.

In every group of six or more that come to dinner, it is reasonable to assume that at least four of them not only dislike you but also the food. You will first begin to notice this right after the soup plates have been cleared. A steady drumming of a knife and fork will be heard. This is to let you know, via the Morse code, that your cook must be drunk. The drumming gets louder as the meal progresses and they finally sign off right after the dessert, informing you, still in code, that they would have dined better had they stayed home and eaten the dog's dinner.

Now it's the guests' privilege to dislike the food. I frequently don't like the food at other people's houses, but when that happens I just quietly stuff myself with bread and hope that the dessert won't be bread pudding. One female food-hater waited until she thought I wasn't watching and then deliberately spilled a lamb chop on my new white rug. I quickly rushed over, brushed off the little chop and, with a courtly bow and a muttered curse, handed it back to her. She thanked me and, after waiting a few minutes, flipped it back again on the rug. This rug (a Polar bear that was still partially alive) began to resemble one of Sonny Liston's opponents right before the *coup de grâce*. I gave her an-

other chop, but this time, before handing it to her, I rolled up the rug and hung it in the closet.

There are guests who, because of their diets, cannot eat certain foods. One gent, a beefy bounder with the gravelly voice of an Atlantic City auctioneer, announced in tones drenched with pride and saliva, that he was full of acid and couldn't eat anything red. This was the night we had roast beef, red cabbage, beets, and watermelon. There he sat, all through the meal, glowering at all the happy and healthy people stuffing themselves with red meat and acid. He accompanied his glowering with a detailed description of his blood pressure, his cholesterol count, and the necessity of seeing his physician at least twice a day. Luckily, he fainted when the watermelon was wheeled in. It seems that in addition to his other ailments he was nearsighted, and mistook the watermelon for the return of the roast beef.

Then there are the couples who never come alone. They always ring in an extra guest, and they are pretty smart about it. The day of the dinner—a sit-down for six—the phone rings about an hour before feeding time and the following conversation takes place:

"This is Jane. I'm terribly sorry but we just can't come to dinner tonight. We have a house guest—an old schoolmate of my husband's. Jack hasn't seen him in fifteen years and we just can't leave him at home." (You find out later why they can't leave him at home. It seems they have a beautiful fifteen-year-old daughter who is an exact copy of Brigitte Bardot, and the way she's been behaving lately, they're not taking any chances.)

So, trapped, you say, "Well, bring him along," hoping he'll get run over by a bus on the way over. "There's always room for one more."

This is true of the Yankee Stadium but it certainly isn't true of the average dining room. However, you squeeze in an extra chair, remove your good service for six and reset the table with a miscellaneous assortment of crockery that you had, over the years, stolen from some of the finest hotels in the country.

To start the evening off with a bang, there is the sneak who always arrives an hour earlier than anyone else. If you say, "Dinner at seven," you can be sure he'll be there at six. If you say "nine," he'll be there at eight. You don't know how he gets in the house—he is either a burglar or a pixie—no one ever hears him come in, no door slams, no bell rings.

Let's say we're dining at seven. At six you go downstairs, unshaved, unbathed, and wearing nothing but a pair of your wife's tennis sneakers. The lights are low—you don't need much light, you know where everything is and, besides, the electric light bills are high enough. You clean the ashes out of the fireplace and you are just in the middle of diluting the whisky with an unequal part of water when you hear a ghostly voice in the gloom.

Your first impulse is to run upstairs and get your revolver, then you suddenly remember that the revolver wouldn't be much good, for you hid the bullets so that the kids wouldn't murder one another. Well, you might as well die defending your home as any other way, so you grab the ice pick, but the room is shaking from the beat of your heart and you are sure he can hear it.

"Did I scare you?" he yells. "It's me, Swanson. I got off early tonight and instead of going all the way home I phoned Martha and told her to meet me here. Why did you put water in the whisky? Is that something new?"

"Don't be silly! Do I look like the type that would put water in the whisky? I was just washing the bottles before sending them back to the liquor store."

You're caught red-handed and there is nothing to do but get out the good bottled-in-bond stuff that you were saving for your golden wedding anniversary.

"If you'll pardon me now, I'll run upstairs and get dressed."

"I'll run up with you," says Swanson. "I could stand a little freshening up. I get pretty dirty at the office and I didn't get a chance to wash." If he had arrived when he was supposed to, he would have had enough time for a bath and a massage.

"Well," you say, "there's a powder room down here. You use that and I'll go upstairs."

You figure that if you can hold him on the main floor you can still knock off that half-hour nap you've been thinking of all afternoon. You wheel sharply and bound up the stairs, but this ghoul comes from a long line of extra speedy ghouls and arrives at the top of the stairs before you do. (At one time he was captain of the track team at Leavenworth.)

"I'll wash with you," he says, "then we can have a little chat before dinner."

For a while you toy with the idea of luring him into the tub and holding his head under water, but that would mean one odd guest at the dinner table. So you kiss the nap good-by and add another name to the long list of chowder heads you hope never to see again.

Then there's the couple who always leaves at midnight but go only as far as the front door. It's practically impossible to get them out of the house—somewhat like a football team that can't make the last three yards. Along about twelve, the husband looks at his watch and in a voice filled with surprise, announces: "Twelve o'clock! Come on, Girlie. I have an early morning appointment."

You quickly rush to the coat closet to help speed the parting guests. That's what you think! There stands the front door, heavy and silent, eager to be flung open to the sounds of happy laughter and merry good nights. But it's no dice—these two are threshold-happy. They're not much fun in the dining or living room, but as their last moments approach, they insist on telling everything!

The wife has found a new beauty parlor and she describes in vivid detail their method of giving a permanent—it's revolutionary and promises to do for straight hair what Eli Whitney did for cotton. This monologue is good for about ten minutes. Now's your chance! You sidle over to the front door and fling it open.

"Well, good night. Will we see you soon?"

Don't be silly—you're going to see them right now and for another hour or so. They haven't begun to commence to start to leave. The husband now closes the front door and says, "Say, did I tell you about the fishing trip we're taking? It's a new lake—only been fished in by Indians—and you know how rarely Indians fish!"

You say, "Yes, isn't it strange that Indians fish so rarely? I guess it's because they don't want to get their papooses wet."

This has no meaning but it distracts their attention and gives you a chance slyly to open the front door with your foot. By this time they have donned their coats and are as comfy as two bugs in a rug. In fact, the cold night air feels kind of good to Mr. and Mrs. Izaak Walton. Mrs. Walton

now proceeds to tell you about a new recipe for salmon salad that she tripped over while disemboweling a horsehair sofa in the attic. This takes fifteen minutes. The hall is now full of a wide assortment of bugs, beetles, and night-flying insects that have been attracted to the entry by the burning light. Around two o'clock, the Waltons begin to run down and, after a few more rounds of good-byes, you finally hustle them through the front door.

Now your work really begins. It takes a good part of an hour, plus the services of the rest of the guests, to round up all the winged and creeping nocturnal creatures zooming through your hallway. Later, in the middle of the night when all is still, the restful sounds of flying bats can be heard fluttering around your bed.

The reluctant thresholders have a running mate in the man who stands up every twenty minutes as though about to depart. Each time he rises, you jump up hopefully and point like a setter toward the coat closet. But you are jumping in vain. This jack-in-the-box isn't leaving for hours! He

has what is known as pantsaphobia. This is a disease that has baffled tailors and psychologists for centuries and can only be cured in the early stages, or (as it is known in the trade) the short-pants period. The disease manifests itself in a complete inability to control the movement of the trouser legs as they creep toward the patient's crotch. What the host imagines to be a desire on the part of the guest to scram is merely a frenzied effort to shake his pants legs back toward his shoe tops.

Then there is the middle-aged harridan (the wife of the interloper who always arrives early) who always blows in just as dinner has been announced, has a quick argument with her husband who is half-looped by this time and, as the hungry diners are about to troop into the dining room, says, "Wait a minute, fellers." (She calls everyone "fellers" regardless of their sex. This is easily understandable, for my guess is she isn't sure what sex she really belongs to.) "Wait a minute, fellers," she bleats, "don't I get a drink?"

"Scotch or bourbon?" you ask politely.

"You know I can't drink whisky," she pouts. "How would you like to fix me a Bomberzine Special?"

What you'd like to do is fix her with a baseball bat, but being the perfect host and unable to remember where you put the bat, you reiterate patiently, "How about some vodka or rye?"

"Don't tell me you never heard of a Bomberzine Special!" She looks at you pityingly. "Well! You don't get around much, do you? Tell me, do you live under a rock?" (At that moment you wouldn't have minded.) "Bomberzines are the only thing the 'in' crowd is drinking. Rubirosa brought it up from the Argentine and you won't believe it but it's just like drinking milk. I had three of them last night and

I had the most exciting dream—all about Paul Anka!"

Just as she is about to reveal the whole dream, you say patiently and with a sort of Mona Lisa smile, "If you'll tell me how it's made I'd be only too happy to fix you one."

"Well," she says, "it's one part Irish whisky, a jigger of rum, one-third grenadine, a touch of Angostura bitters, a spoonful of pomegranate, and ten drops of whipped cream."

You counter with, "How about some chocolate-covered Seconals?"

"If it's too much trouble," she answers witheringly, "I'll fix it myself."

Before you can head her off, she is in the kitchen, dripping with pomegranate juice and whipped cream, shoving the food around, shouting at the cook, and otherwise helping to ruin forty-eight dollars' worth of groceries!

Another nice little special is the lone-wolf, squirrel-like guest. He comes alone; he comes early; he is nut-happy. He whiles away the hours before dinner by crunching his way through a whole bowl of peanuts. Then, half-stuffed, he coasts through dinner. Nothing much—just a little caviar and perhaps an odd truffle or two. Once the meal is over, however, he slips into high. His high happens to be pistachio nuts, and how that boy can make them disappear at a dollar-sixty a pound! Give him a large bowl of pistachio nuts and a Bach fugue and the world is his!

He has his own special technique. He doesn't simply place the nuts in his mouth the way his two-footed friends do. He knows that if he did, he'd be expelled from the squirrels' union. He eats them the right way, and the right way is to crack them noisily with his teeth, then, with his hand about eight inches from his mouth, he tosses the nuts into his craw with a steady motion somewhat like a stoker firing a freight train up a steep grade. He never misses—his aim is uncanny! Once all the available nuts have disappeared he jumps up abruptly and streaks out, probably to spend the night in a tree.

The simplest methods are usually the most effective in getting rid of week-end guests. A few well-placed remarks during dinner will, as a rule, do the trick. For example, when the roast is brought in you can complain, "Meat is certainly getting expensive! It's not easy to keep a family going these days, to say nothing of guests."

When you come to the last part of this speech, glare at the guest. If he has any pride at all (and very few of them have) he will go to his room and immediately start packing. If, however, he is the usual week-ender, such subtleties are a waste of time and stronger methods must be devised, even up to and including force.

It is never wise to use violence unless the guest is a woman or a very small man. (In inviting guests, it is a good idea to keep this in mind; always try to get the tiniest people you possibly can.) If, however, you happen to be stuck with normal-sized people, there are many little tricks that can be used. Cutting off the water supply and snipping the telephone wires is usually effective. Burning their mail (particularly if it's the kind I get) sometimes helps. A good many people are allergic to crackers in bed, especially the old-fashioned soda or oyster cracker, and are usually willing to depart after rising in the morning resembling a breaded veal cutlet. (One guest, however, was so delighted with this treatment that he ate the crackers every night before going to sleep, and after a week of this, unpacked all his things and began shouting through the keyhole for cheese.)

If any of my friends read this and recognize themselves in this essay, remember, I am only kidding. And if they want me to take them to dinner, how about tomorrow night at Joe's Coffee Pot, corner Fifth and Main, six o'clock sharp?

2

How I Beat the Social Game

 I'm not going to kid anybody. There was a time when, if I found myself staring at four or five assorted forks at a formal dinner table, I was in a quandary. But that was long before the Four Hundred became the Four Hundred and One and I became known as the Elsa Maxwell of Hollywood.

Friends who used to laugh when I sat down at the dinner table now flock to me for advice on etiquette. Hostesses rush to the telephone to ask what kind of wine should be served with the wienies, or where to place the guest of honor who has just put three spoons in his pocket. But the nicest compliment of all came from Amy Vanderbilt herself. Watching me in action at a fashionable dinner she admitted that, in comparison with me, she knew nothing about etiquette. Her exact words, as I recall them, were, "If that Mr. Marx knows anything about etiquette, I'm a monkey's uncle!"

And yet, even applause and adulation can become tiresome. It becomes inconvenient to have people barge up to you at all hours, asking how you managed to lick the social game—especially if at the moment you happen to be kissing the hand of a White Russian duchess. (I'm sure she was a White Russian duchess because I've never met a colored one.)

I could, of course, refer people to the standard books on

etiquette, but I'm afraid they're of little practical value to a man who lives, as I do, without a footman, three wines at dinner, and caviar for breakfast. What I have accomplished is simply the result of observing a few simple rules and keeping my nose clean.

It is a matter of record that in 1959 I attended 336 parties, with invitations to more than twelve of them. Of course you have to invite people to your house, too. But I won't give much space to that because, with a little careful planning, you can see to it that their invitations reach them when they're out of town.

As I say, this requires careful planning. Once, when I was in New York, I gave a dinner party for twelve friends who, according to the newspapers, were attending a convention in Minneapolis. Well, it so happened that the papers were wrong. Only four of them had gone to the convention. The other eight came to my house and, please believe me, they were even more disgusted than I was with the carelessness of modern journalism. There was nothing in the house but some cat food, and I didn't even have a cat.

I wasn't home myself that evening because I was an unexpected dinner guest in Brooklyn. I mention that because it brings up a point that has been neglected by every other authority on etiquette. I refer to the uninvited guest, or as the vulgarians phrase it, the crasher.

My advice is this: If your host has, for some reason or other, neglected to invite you to the party you're attending, do not embarrass him by calling his attention to that fact. Only a very low person would enter a home uninvited and say, "You're a fine one! Throwing a party and not asking me! I had a good notion not to come."

Under the circumstances, a gentleman enters the house

blithely, through the front door rather than an upstairs window (which I consider the worst kind of social climbing).

He will not make an immediate dash for the bar. Not only because this sort of thing is crude, but because "party liquor," generally of an inferior grade, is served there. I have found that if you slip the butler a buck or two he will get you the stuff he (and of course the host) drink themselves.

Since clothes make the man, a woman ought to give a lot of thought to her dress. Her host will inform her whether or not she's expected to appear in formal attire. And he should take pains to be specific, because I know a member of one of New York's first families (first as you drive up Tenth Avenue) who wrote on his invitation, "We're not dressing." Unfortunately, one of his guests, a charming and attractive lady, took this a bit too literally. (What do I mean "unfortunately?")

As a general rule, a woman makes no mistake in wearing a simple afternoon gown in the afternoon and a nightgown at night. With men, dress is even less of a problem. A black tie is always appropriate, provided you're wearing a collar. Tails, in my estimation, look good only on dogs.

The experienced diner-out generally manages to be the first one at the table so that, in the event he has been seated next to a cluck, he can switch the place cards. If discovered doing this, the gentleman will not, of course, make snide remarks about the cluck. Instead he will adopt a more constructive attitude, gaily tossing off some such observation as, "I simply must sit next to the Countess Rittenhouse. The boys at the club tell me she's loads of fun once you pour a few beers in her." (It is extremely bad form to accompany

this remark with a leering, "Eh, Countess?")

Now to the food—and about time, too. The first thing to bear in mind is that the salad is at your left, and, unless it's asparagus, should not be touched with your fingers. The dish at your right (Countess Rittenhouse) should not be touched at all.

In dining out and finding the food unsatisfactory, a gentleman does not grumble and say that he could have had a better meal at home without having to wait until eight forty-five for it. And he certainly will not make threatening remarks, such as, "Madame, if this schnitzel gives me ptomaine, you'll hear from my lawyers in the morning." (If he does get ptomaine, he strives to make a friendly settlement.) But all of that can be avoided by smiling at the hostess and saying, "Ella, darling, I managed the soup and salad, but this swill has me licked. How about rustling me up a couple of eggs?"

Of all the good things in life, nothing is more popular than necking. (If any teen-agers are reading this they will please substitute the current expression for that pastime.) The real gentleman does not indulge in this practice indiscriminately. He will never neck in a ballroom unless the dance floor is crowded, and he will make no attempt to kiss a young lady who has just yelled for a policeman. Obviously, a man in uniform has more romantic appeal than the rest of us in business suits.

Most young women do not welcome promiscuous advances. (Either that, or my luck's been terrible.) In society they must learn how to keep a gentleman from pawing without offending him. For that I recommend flattery—some such personal remark as, "Did anyone ever tell you that you resemble a weasel?"

And now let's see if you've been paying attention.

If, while carving a turkey, you drop it into the lap of the dowager at your right, do you:

(a) apologize profusely;

(b) break into tears; or

(c) say, "Madame, I have not given you the bird; I'll thank you to fork it over immediately"?

Should chives or parsley be served with a steak on a black eye?

Is it proper to use a nickname—say, Stinky—on your

calling cards, assuming that nobody ever calls you Roderick?

If you ask a young woman for a dance and she tells you her feet hurt—then, thirty seconds later, you see her waltzing away with a young man who has more vaseline on his hair (also more hair), do you ask her for an introduction to her chiropodist, or do you pretend you're dead?

When the lady grabs the check in a restaurant, should she slip the dough under the table to the gentleman or openly hand it to the waiter?

On leaving a nightclub that's been raided, who enters the wagon first—the lady or the gentleman?

When a young couple dining out has a spat, should the husband put his best foot forward or wait until he has a pair of spats?

Describe the design and colors of three of Lucius Beebe's vests.

How can you get a songwriter away from the piano at a party without blasting?

If you can answer seven of the foregoing questions incorrectly, and have eaten the tops of four cereal boxes, write in for your Society Man Badge.

And when would you like me to drop in at your house for dinner some evening?

3

The Pariah of Hollywood Am I

The Hollywood social ladder is a high and dizzy one, and right below the bottom rung, if you look closely, you will find . . . well, just read on.

It's eleven o'clock at night and I am sitting up in bed with the assorted works of Sir Walter Scott and a glass of warm milk. Don't get the idea that I have been in bed all evening. As a matter of fact, I have just returned from a dinner party. There were six people present, including the hostess and her husband. Before dinner we each had a glass of sherry and after dinner we each had a cordial and a two-hour conversation. The men discussed politics, the traffic problem, and the women. The women talked about their hair, the Parent Teachers Association, and the men. By ten-thirty the yawning became pretty general and by eleven I was home in bed.

After thirty years in Hollywood, I have slowly and reluctantly come to the conclusion that I am a social bust. I am finally convinced that I must have most of the physical curses that the television commercials loudly assure you they can cure in twenty-four hours. Only in this way can I explain the cloistered existence that I lead in a town that is famous for its hoopla and merriment.

I never seem to crash the sets that the columnists are always writing about. Oh, my name appears frequently in some columns, but it's usually in connection with a television show I am about to appear in or some other theatrical plan I am contemplating. I never see my name in a movie column when a party like the following has been thrown:

> Mr. and Mrs. Basil Metabolism entertained three hundred and sixty couples at a garden party to welcome the return of Steve Gwendolyn from a trip to Peru. A satin tent covered the entire three acres, and, as each couple arrived, they were given a miniature swimming pool and a keg of champagne. *Life* magazine covered the event and had its cameras focused mainly on the starlets with the most abbreviated bikinis. At eleven o'clock a mock auction was held and the hostess' daughter was sold to a used-car dealer who jokingly said he planned on trading her in on a new Rolls Royce. Kim and Frankie breezed in around 1:00 A.M. and kept everyone enthralled singing the works of Burl Ives. Around 3:00 A.M. naked girls were shot out of cannons into the waiting arms of those lucky ones who were baching it, and it wasn't until the sun crept over the hills that the orgy finally broke up.

Just as wolves travel in packs, this town travels in sets, and if you are not a definite part of one of these cliques you'll find yourself at home in the evening, repairing the washing machine, the television set, or trying to wheedle a big ship into a small bottle.

For example, there is the gambling set. They depart each day at noon for one of the race tracks, equipped with binoculars, racing forms and a covey of blondes. They can't name all of the fifty states but they can rattle off the names of all the nags running that day at the major tracks. This crowd improves each shining hour. They play gin rummy on the way to the track and gin rummy on the way home from the track. After they have eaten dinner they play gin rummy until it's time to go to the track again. In the winter, if they are lucky enough to have a divorce pending, they journey to Las Vegas or Reno. Here they can discard an old wife or husband, latch onto a new one, and play gin rummy at the same time. They are always on the move. They are either flying back from Mexico City or planing to Jamaica. When they tire of gambling they repair to the night clubs and hot spots. These cafés are famous for their brawls and in many of the places white tie and brass knuckles are obligatory. About once a week the following can be found in any of the syndicated columns:

> Devereaux Barrett, singing star of *Death Valley Days*, wound up on the wrong end of a gin bottle last night at the Copacadero. In court this morning, sporting a shiner, he testified that it was all a mistake. He said he was under a table, trying to give his fiancée a hotfoot, but the place was so jammed that he didn't realize he was applying the torch to the wife of a prominent mining engineer who had just passed out at an adjoining table.

Here it is—life, love, and laughter. And what am I doing while all this is going on? I'm home drying cherry pits to make a bean bag for my cook's nephew.

I'm a little old for the athletic set, but even in my heyday, when my arteries were as soft as my head, I don't think I could have survived this crowd. They've never invited me, but it's just as well. They're up at the crack of dawn, galloping over mountain trails and streams. After a hasty breakfast, while still in the saddle, they whip their foam-crested steeds back to the stable and dive into somebody's swimming pool. They don't care whose pool it is. They are in and out so fast that nobody recognizes them anyway. After this, five sets of tennis, a drive to the ocean for a quick dip, and then some handball before dinner. After dining they usually play Ping-pong until it's time to hop into the saddle again. While these supermen are galloping over hill and dale, I'm stumbling around the bathroom groping for any small white pellet that might conceivably send me off to dreamland.

Even the intellectual crowd will have none of me. Physically, I look like one of them. Graying at the temples, I walk with a slight limp and wear thick glasses. But I have been tried and found wanting. Through a mistake that has never been explained, I was invited to one of their dinner parties. On receipt of the invitation I rushed down to the public library and boned up on a dozen assorted subjects. I poked around Plato, scratched around Spinoza, and read *Finnegan's Wake* frontward and backward. (I understood it better backward.) By the night of the party I was sure I knew enough to muddle through the evening. I know better now. This was a writers' crowd. Most of the women had short hair and thick socks and most of the men had ulcers and no socks. Until the lights were turned on full blast for the games, it wasn't easy to distinguish between the sexes.

I was still wiping the fruit cup stains off my vest when the hostess herded us all into the living room and quickly outfitted us with pencils and paper. They then chose sides and bombarded one another with questions that would have withered the combined brains of Bertrand Russell, Nathan Pusey, and Arthur Schlesinger, Sr. *and* Jr. After a few preliminary intellectual skirmishes they let me off the hook and I slunk back to the kitchen to resume rubbing the fruit stains off my vest.

There are many other groups and sets in Hollywood. They differ in many ways but they all have one thing in common: they avoid me. I'm just a lonely beachcomber on the town's social sea.

I must admit that I'm discouraged, but I'm determined that some day I'll crash Hollywood society. If all else fails, I'll sit in my car on Sunset Boulevard and, for a small fee, I'll show the tourists the outside of all the houses that I'm never invited into.

4

Adventures of an Extra Man

Some years ago Clare Boothe Luce was our Ambassador to Italy and I was a movie actor. I met her one night at a fashionable dinner party. The only reason I was invited was because the host owed me three hundred dollars from an old crap game, and since I knew I would never get the money I decided I would take what I could get in free meals.

Mrs. Luce was there alone and so was I. She was staying with friends in Bel Air and they had dropped her off. About one in the morning the party started breaking up and the host asked me if I would mind taking Mrs. Luce home. Rather warily I asked, "Where is she staying?"

"Oh, somewhere in Bel Air," he replied.

"Delighted," I said. "Lovely place, Bel Air."

Our host said, "Well, it's rather foggy tonight. I hope you won't get lost."

"Me? Lost? Don't give it another thought. I know that

section like a mother knows her child. Don't forget, I'm practically a native of California." I don't know why I said that except that, basically, I'm a braggart and never overlook an opportunity to make myself seem important.

I had never had an ambassador in my car, either male or female, and turning to Mrs. Luce I said, with all the innate gallantry which, since childhood, has distinguished me from the *canaille*, "I would be honored to drive one so eminent to her destination."

I thought Mrs. Luce winced a little at this inane statement, but perhaps it was just my imagination.

I have lived in California since 1930, or to put it another way, I blew New York right after the market crashed. I might add that I had just enough money left to make it by unchartered bus. Nevertheless, despite the thirty-odd years I've lived here, there are certain sections of town that throw me. Five minutes in that labyrinth called Bel Air and I might just as well be deep in the heart of the Solomon Islands. Whether it's because I wear bifocals or because I haven't had my glasses changed since Coolidge was in office, my sense of direction is more than a little off-center. If Daniel Boone were alive today he would get a lot of laughs watching me as I flounder my way through a strange neighborhood.

For example, last week while dining at a prominent hotel, I walked through a door to what I thought was the men's room, only to realize that if the creatures flying out of there in a panic were men, they were dressing rather peculiarly these days.

Bel Air, I am convinced, was laid out by some diabolic sadist who deliberately decided not to use a compass or a surveyor. He is gone now, to that Great Map Maker up in the sky, but in my mind's eye I see him sitting high in a tower overlooking what he hath wrought and laughing hysterically as he watches through his field glasses the plight of his victims as they helplessly crisscross and overlap each other on their different routes to limbo. For example, if you took two dozen cooked noodles and carelessly threw them on a cracked plate and then threw the whole thing out the window, you would have a fairly accurate idea of how the roads are laid out. To add to the bewilderment of the befuddled driver, about ten at night a thick pall of fog rolls in from the blue Pacific and completely envelops this rustic little piece of real estate.

Well, we set off bravely and within five minutes we were as completely lost as though we were in the Upper Nile. An hour of aimless driving went by. In that hour we discussed our host; we dabbled in politics; and we reviewed the entire world scene, sector by sector.

Mrs. Luce is a brilliant conversationalist, and as my dialogue grew increasingly incoherent I could sense that she was looking forward to getting away from me. Like most women who have achieved success, she is practical and perceptive. Just as I was half way through explaining why Rembrandt's paintings would never live, she stopped me with, "Mr. Marx, I don't want to criticize your driving or your sense of direction, but if you will pardon my bluntness, I don't believe you have the faintest idea where we are. Do you think it might be a good idea to stop at some corner and look at the street sign on a lamp post?"

Scenically, Bel Air is unquestionably one of the garden spots of the world. Even the lamp posts are surrounded by a fairly high ornamental hedge to conceal the mundane fact that they do not float in the air but are fastened to the side-

walk in the same manner as the lamp posts in Dubuque or Weekok.

The fog was growing heavier and the visibility had decreased to about ten feet. I took the hint and stopped the car at the next corner. We both climbed out of the car and, prodded by my companion, I shinnied up the post as though to the manner born. Here my years in the navy stood me in good stead.

I read the name of the street. "Mrs. Luce," I called down,

"you have nothing more to worry about. I now know precisely where we are. Furthermore, I would like to take this occasion, while I'm up here, to apologize for losing my way. The fact is, I was so engrossed in your fascinating appraisal of world affairs that I must confess I neglected my driving just a wee bit."

I gracefully shinnied down the pole and, as we stood there in that clump of wet bushes, out of the fog emerged a figure. I recognized the face. It belonged to Charles Brackett, producer and writer at Twentieth Century–Fox studio. Mr. Brackett resides in Bel Air and is a part-time insomniac who makes a ritual of walking his mutt (which, for some curious reason, he insists is a French Poodle) through the hills every morning at two. This will give you some idea of the fascinating life the average movie producer lives in this sequestered section.

Mr. Brackett is a man of great dignity, and his composure is rarely shaken, but I must say he looked a little startled, if not alarmed, to see these two shrouded figures standing there in the soggy hedge. He surveyed us for a moment, unwilling to believe his eyes, then turned and addressed his dog. "Spyros," he said, "up to now I thought I'd seen everything, but if someone had told me I would ever see the United States Ambassador to Italy and Groucho Marx standing in a bush in Bel Air at two in the morning, I just wouldn't have believed it!" He then doffed his hat to Mrs. Luce and patiently directed us out of this maze which, had it been smaller, could have been used for training rats. Mr. Brackett then turned and disappeared into the gloom.

Mrs. Luce said cheerfully, "Well, Mr. Marx, with these instructions we should be home in five minutes."

What she didn't know is that I have absolutely no powers

of concentration and had already forgotten everything Mr. Brackett had just told me.

In the meantime, the friends with whom Mrs. Luce had been staying became worried about her prolonged absence and had phoned our host of the evening. He informed them that we had left his house at one A.M. and should certainly have reached their home by 1:15. Alarmed, they phoned the police who promptly dispatched two prowl cars to comb the area. At 4:40 A.M. they found us. Mrs. Luce was standing in a clump of wet bushes and I, as usual, was perched on top of another lamp post.

I trust it was just coincidence, but the next day Mrs. Luce departed for Italy and I went back to MGM. In all the intervening years, for some reason or other, she never asked me to escort her home again.

5

A Spirited Evening
at Home

With the possible exception of clothes, beauty salons, and Frank Sinatra, there are few subjects all women agree upon. One of the topics that seems to hold an unholy fascination for all of them is mysticism. Crystal balls, gypsy fortune tellers, tea leaves, palm readers, séances, and even messages in Chinese fortune cookies can hold them in thrall. All of which goes to prove that the female is only about fifteen years removed from the jungle. This, however, is part of their charm, along with high heels, nylons, a bulging bra, and even, white teeth.

I've seen them sit for hours, feverish and bug-eyed, around an irregular piece of lumber called a Ouija Board. If you dared tell them they were doing the shoving themselves, without any help from supernatural forces, they would bare their pearly teeth and order you to shut up and clear out.

When I first came to Hollywood I lived in an old, dusty house in the hills. In those days there was no television to assist one in ruining an evening, and other ways had to be found to while away the long, dreary nights between dinner parties. Sex had been discovered and abandoned by most of my friends.

One evening a quartette of my friends' wives were sitting in front of the huge fireplace in our living room. These were routine middle-aged babes with grown children and touched-up hair. What were they doing? They were intently pushing a small wooden object that resembled a punctured kidney round and round a Ouija Board.

It was a warm evening and there was nothing in the fireplace but some old, wrinkled newspaper left over from the previous winter, and a few semiburned logs. There they sat, those silly women, pushing that daffy object up and down and around. They were goggle-eyed with excitement. Not even an earthquake could have distracted them.

I finally walked over and, in a friendly voice, asked what all the excitement was about. One of them told me to shut up. Another witty one said, "Drop dead!" The third just muttered, "Go away, you fool!" The fourth explained, through clenched teeth, "If you must know, stupid, we are getting spirit signals from George Washington!"

George Washington? If they had said George Raft, I might have understood. But Washington? He's been dead almost two hundred years (and probably busier now than he ever was), but here were these four feeble-minded housewives, feverishly trying to get in touch with him. I could understand their trying to reach Martha, but what could George possibly have in common with them?

Round and round the board these ancient virgins continued to shove the hunk of wood. Finally, one said, "George, we are trying to reach you. Are you getting our signal? Do you hear us?"

I don't know if George heard them, but a medium-sized mouse suddenly scurried out of the fireplace. The four women screamed and leaped for the top of the piano.

Somehow, I never could convince them that that mouse wasn't the father of our country. And the way things are going today, perhaps he is.

6

A Night on the Town, Medium Rare

Years ago, when we lived on the South Side of Chicago, it had become a fairly good-sized slum. Most of the wealthier natives had long since scrammed, either going farther south or taking one of the North Side roads which, if you weren't careful, would eventually wind up in Milwaukee.

As most of the big, stately homes became increasingly mouldy and run-down, they were taken over by tailors, plumbers, dressmakers, real estate sharks, ladies of easy virtue, and other live-wire enterprises. One of these gamey brownstones housed a spiritualist. Her handbills were flung all over the South Side. Lawns were inundated with her throw-aways. I don't remember the exact wording but they had a nice comforting tone. In large, scarlet letters they said, "Would you like to communicate with your loved ones even though they are no longer in the flesh? Remember, your dear departed miss you. Let us help you commune with them. There are no questions about the hereafter that cannot be answered. Every night from 8:30 to 11:00 at Mystic Hall." The address followed and it was signed, "Madame Ali Ben Mecca, Arabia's Leading Exponent of the Occult Arts."

From past experience and many years of domestic warfare I knew it was only a question of time before I would be obliged to attend one of these séances. I would have been much smarter had I consented to go when it was first mentioned. It would have eliminated weeks of wrangling, recrimination, and vocal counterpunching.

We arrived just as the large, dingy room was filling up. On the altar incense was burning in two large urns. It was one of the most peculiar odors I had ever inhaled. Having played small-time vaudeville for years, I quickly diagnosed this stink as a rather odd blend of opium, cauliflower, dog acts, and toilet water. My first impulse was to faint. However, my female companion, a veteran of long years of internecine warfare and bargain-hunting, quickly dragged me over to a low stool and began fanning me. She had some difficulty bringing me to, but finally solved the problem by kicking me steadily in the shins.

Shaking myself like a Newfoundland dog just emerging from the water, I saw standing by the shrine a tall, anemic-looking Zombie, attired in a Russian general's uniform topped off with a high silk hat. He cautioned us all to be patient. In silvery tones he explained that, before making her appearance, it was necessary for the Madame to attune her ectoplasm to the spirit world. He babbled on like this for quite some time as the semideadly fumes continued to belch from the two urns, seemingly determined to put me to sleep. The little lady at my side (an early wife) was just as determined to keep me awake. It became a contest. Each time I got a deep whiff of that perfumed stench my head began to sag. Seeing this, she would instantly deliver a crashing kick to the shins. In very short order I was not only drugged but my ankles were beginning to acquire the color of an old meerschaum pipe.

Suddenly I heard a loud clang of cymbals and the Madame from Arabia blew in, all three hundred pounds of her. She wore a diaphanous outfit with a long train that was held up by her two olive-skinned attendants. The Madame may have been from Arabia, as advertised, but to a man who traveled extensively for many years through the South, she bore a striking resemblance to Aunt Jemima. All she needed to complete the picture was a box of pancake flour in her hands. Her entrance brought a sharp poke in the ribs from my adversary, and before I knew what I was doing I had dropped three dollars in an earthen pot which one of the subsidiary thieves was toting around the room.

The fat Arabian seeress now having been seated with all the ceremony befitting one of her exalted rank, the barker announced that the three bucks we had all dropped into the pot entitled us to absolutely nothing in the way of astral communication. He solemnly explained that this was just the admittance fee, but added that for an extra five dollars the Madame would get in touch with any friend or relative who was lucky enough to have kicked the bucket. Throwing caution to the winds and eager for the additional five bucks he said, "If you have no dearly departed, Madame will answer any question, no matter what the subject—the stock market, the results of any sporting event, how long you will live, or any other information you are seeking. The Queen sees all and knows all."

At the mention of another five dollars, groggy as I was, I instinctively started to grope my way to the exit. My fair companion, rising to the occasion, grabbed me by the seat of the trousers and jerked me back to the milking stool on which I had been squatting for the past hour. "Where do you think you're going?" she snarled.

"I'm getting the hell out of here," I replied.

"Oh no, you're not! You sit right there and put up the other five dollars, you miser!"

"Look," I whined, "I'm stuck for three dollars now. Why should I throw in another five bucks? She's got nothing to say that I want to hear." I discovered that by not breathing at all, I was once again able to think clearly.

"You may not have anything to ask her," she said smugly, "but I have. I came here to commune with my aunt's husband. He was my favorite uncle and he's been dead for eight years. He keeps sending me messages. Some nights we vibrate together."

I was considered quite witty in those days and I replied, "Why don't you write him a letter? Write it on asbestos. You know where he is."

"Ho, ho," she said, "that's very funny. You'd be a riot in a small night club. Now put in the five dollars!"

In the meantime, Aunt Jemima had slipped off into slumberland. In soft, soothing terms the barker then announced that although her material body was still seated on the imperial throne, her astral body was flying around in Never-Never Land. He added that when she returned from her long journey all those who had dropped five dollars in the pot were entitled to question her about the after life, their present life, or their future life.

As he concluded this pitch, Madame Mecca's eyes began

to open, her two page boys began fanning the incense pots and the perfumed smog was now reaching the stage that, today in Los Angeles, calls for an alert.

The first dupe to throw a question was a withered trollop with a face like a Halloween mask. She said that her husband wasn't dead but that he had disappeared, and when would he return? Well, sir, you didn't have to be a fortune teller to know the answer to that one! One look at her and you knew he was never coming back. How she ever got him in the first place was the mystery.

The Madame then consulted with the barker, and after a few minutes of muffled abracadabra the seeress announced that the gargoyle's husband would definitely return within the next ten years. Since the woman who had asked the question was about sixty, I didn't see how that was going to do her much good.

My companion then raised her hand to indicate that she had a question to ask, but even in my stupor I was quicker than she was and got my hand up first. "You say your Queen can answer any question asked of her?" I demanded.

"That's right," answered the barker.

"Even if it's not about the dead?"

"Madame Mecca has never failed to answer any question," he assured me.

"Okay, then. What's the capital of North Dakota?"

The Madame and her consort seemed stunned, dismayed, and bewildered. This was one hell of a thing to ask someone who had just returned from another world! She sat there, rigid, then turned to the Prince. He apparently had encountered problems of this kind before. The world was full of skeptics, but he had a ready solution. Beckoning to the two stooges who were busily fanning the incense pots, he bent over and whispered a few hasty instructions. I don't know what he said but it seemed to make them very happy. The next thing I knew, they each lifted me by one elbow and hustled me to the front door. I kept shouting for my five dollars and also for the police (in that order), but I guess the police were busy that night robbing a bank or two. At any rate, no one came to my rescue. They shoved me out the iron door and quickly slammed it behind me.

I sat down on the stone steps and gratefully breathed in the comparatively fresh air of Chicago's South Side. An hour later my female companion appeared. Her eyes were shining and in an hysterically high soprano she triumphantly announced that, through the medium, she had spoken with her dead uncle. "He told me that he was happy as a lark," she enthused.

"I can understand that," I said. "That's because his wife is still up here!"

Part Four

It Happened
to Eight
Other Guys

1

Scars Without Wounds

The government's attitude toward the theatrical profession has always been a curious one. An actor has nothing but his body, his talent, and his personal magnetism, and when these wear out he is just a memory that is soon forgotten. This applies to prize fighters, baseball players, and athletes in general.

If a man owns a grocery store or a butcher shop and he becomes ill, he can hire someone to replace him. If an actor is sick, his income stops immediately.

So, be smart. Don't go into show business. Buy an oil well or a few hundred acres of timber. Don't buy anything the government won't subsidize or allow you to depreciate.

For years the theatrical unions have tried to persuade the government to allow actors to deduct something for the wear and tear on their carcasses, but apparently the pressure the unions were able to exert wasn't enough to force the politicos in Washington to do anything about it.

In wartime no group is quicker to volunteer its services. The automobile factories, the aircraft manufacturers, and all the other industries grow pretty fat on their wartime profits. The actor gets his expenses, ten or eleven miserly dollars a day, and when the war is over they hand him a plaque.

Now that I've got that off my chest, along with most of my curly hair, let us be specific.

There was a beautiful young female star who turned down a couple of juicy contracts because she was a patriot who wanted to do her bit for the war effort. Like most pretty women she was, to put it mildly, a flirt. Her husband, a tall, cadaverous, balding writer, was violently jealous, both of her beauty and of her millions of admirers.

One day she came home and told him she had heard the call of duty and decided she was going to tour the army camps. She added that she would probably be away for at least two months. This jolly piece of news damned near put him in shock. Noticing the tragic expression on his face, she tried to soften the blow. "Don't worry, honey," she reassured him, "I know I'll be awfully busy, but I promise I'll drop you a postcard every day or so."

"A postcard!" he thought. This was certainly not much of a substitute for one of the world's most desirable women! If you have ever received a postcard you know that it is sexless, short, and flat. His wife, on the other hand, was tall, voluptuous, exquisite, and fascinating. He looked at her with eyes full of love and venom.

"Do you expect me to go to bed every night, satisfied with just looking at a lousy postcard from some army base?" he shouted. "If I wanted a postcard to love, I'd have married one!"

This didn't make much sense, but she didn't become angry. She realized that the news had sent his mind whirling into the wild blue yonder. Being a woman, she was naturally pleased that he loved her so much and desired her so passionately.

He was convinced, however, that if she went touring with fifteen or sixteen actors and appeared nightly before all those handsome, sex-starved officers, there was a good chance she would either come home with child, or, what was even worse, not at all. It wasn't that she didn't love him, but she loved all men, and men found her just as irresistible as she did them.

Her husband tried for days to talk her out of this adventure, but she was not only patriotic—she was basically a nymphomaniac. She paid little attention to his tearful entreaties.

He not only loved her madly, but like many husbands who are married to beautiful tootsies, he didn't trust her any farther than a midget could throw a piano. All his pleadings were to no avail. She simply repeated, "I love my country and I'm going to do all I can to lift the spirits of those poor boys who are giving their all!"

This last statement frightened her husband beyond belief, but finally realizing that he was getting nowhere, he decided on a new approach. "My dear," he said gently, "are you planning to sing and dance on this tour?"

"No, darling," she said. "Do you remember that murder mystery we saw on Broadway a few seasons ago? It was called *Mr. and Mrs. North,* and the big scene is in the second act where someone opens a closet door and a corpse falls out, face down, right on the stage. Well, that's the play we're going to do. The boys will love it."

As she unfolded the plot, a fantastic idea flitted through his wily mind. "About that corpse, dear, is that all the actor does in the whole play, just fall out of a closet onto the floor?"

"Well, almost," she said. "He does have a few lines of dialogue in the first act, but anyone could play it."

"Fine," he beamed. "Now look, darling, I'm a writer and a writer can work anywhere. I can write just as well at some army or navy base as I can at the studio. Now then, I have a wonderful idea. I'll play the corpse and then we can be together all the time. Night and day!"

As soon as she heard this she realized she had made a monstrous *gaffe*. If she had only kept her pretty mouth shut!

"I think," he purred, "when two people are as much in love as we are, they should never be apart. You know the old saw, 'Absence makes the heart grow fonder . . . for somebody else.' " He laughed heartily, but he laughed alone.

She was stuck. Tricky as she was, she couldn't find any device to extricate herself from this web he was subtly weaving around her. In fairness to the young lady I don't mean to imply that she had volunteered to entertain the troops just to get away from her husband, but since she was going to make this sacrifice for the fighting men, on land or sea, she didn't see any reason why she couldn't get a little extracurricular fun out of it herself.

A few days later they went into rehearsal. The first time they ran through the play the husband fell out of the closet with all the éclat of an early Barrymore. No corpse, alive or dead, could have done it more realistically. The director was delighted and showered him with praise. He even suggested he abandon writing as a career and become an actor.

However, since he wasn't accustomed to falling out of closets, this role shook him up quite a bit. The third day he cornered the director and said, "Look, old boy, since we're going to be rehearsing this thing another two weeks, how about placing a mattress in front of the closet? I'm not crazy about getting banged up needlessly."

"All right," said the director, "but just for the rehearsals. You understand that when we do this in front of an audience, it has to be realistic."

Fourteen days later they opened at a naval base in Oak-

land, California. All went well, and when the closet door opened and the corpse fell out, the audience yelled in terror. The opening was a resounding success. Everyone loved the actors and the entire performance.

The husband was so happy to be with his loved one that when he undressed that night he hardly noticed the pain in his back. The next evening when the closet door opened, he did a beautiful fall. Again the audience shrieked at the shock of a dead body falling before them. That night when he retired he had a substantial lump on his forehead and the pain in his back was worse. The third night when he fell out of the closet, his left knee gave way. At the finish of the fourth performance he was rushed to the base hospital.

The navy doctor, after examining him, announced that he had dislocated his spine and it would be necessary to put him in traction. He added that it would be some months before the hospital could release him.

Husband and wife are back together now. He walks with a slight limp and a cane and tells everyone that he got it from being in the war. This isn't true. He really got it from being in love.

2

Calling with a Full House

He's middle-aged now, but in his twenties he was quite a pixie and playboy. He liked women but his love was poker. As they grew older most of his card-playing friends married and found other ways of amusing themselves, and if you've ever been married you know that when love comes in freedom usually flies out the window.

Alex wasn't the marrying kind. He often said he'd never met a girl who could give him as much pleasure as a good poker hand. However he was finding it increasingly difficult to round up enough players for one of those wonderful evenings they used to have, shut up in a small, cozy room reeking of cigars, cigarettes, pipe tobacco, beer, and booze. Even though the stench is appalling, a stag card room seems to bring out the man in the average man. I think it's because it's one of the few remaining retreats from the average woman's dialogue.

For Alex, no girl he ever fondled could match the sensation and thrill he felt when he touched a deck of cards. He was a charming gambler. When he lost, he lost the same way he won—with a smile. Naturally, he preferred winning to losing, but that wasn't the most important thing. What he loved was the company of his poker-playing pals and the game itself.

It was a rainy night in December and Alex hadn't played poker in weeks. He was all alone by the telephone, so he began calling up his single friends. He had picked a bad night. Most of them had dates. Desperate, he called his married friends, but they all had wives. One of the wives got on the phone and said, "Alex, Joe would love to come, but we promised mother we'd drop in on her tonight. We're going to play Mah Jong with matchsticks. We don't play for money. You see, mother is a Seventh Day Adventist and they aren't allowed to gamble, except for nothing."

This was depressing enough, but there was more to come. Another husband had to baby-sit while his wife attended a bridge tournament. A third wife explained, "Fred would be delighted to play, Alex, but you won't believe this, right

now Fred is in the kitchen drying the dishes. I've never told this to anyone before," she giggled, "and if he knew I was telling you, he'd kill me, but when he proposed to me he promised that if I would marry him he would always help me with the dishes. Of course it really isn't important that he dry the dishes, but I consider it's his way of showing how much he loves me."

Alex didn't know whether to hang up or throw up. He finally compromised by doing both. Now he was really in a dilemma. He despised playing cards with women, but desperate times require desperate measures. So he picked up the phone and called a lady friend of his who had more girls than you could shake a stick at. This isn't what the girls were generally used for, but no matter.

This lady friend was the madam of the most luxurious sporting house in Hollywood, and Alex had been a steady customer there for years.

"Hello, Eden, this is Alex. How's business?"

"Well, you know, Alex," she said, "with the rain and the taxes, things are just awful around here."

"That's fine, then there'll be no problem. Could you send three girls over to my house right away? It's an emergency."

"Three girls!" the madam laughed. "Why, Alex, you must be taking some of those new hormones."

"Don't be witty, Eden, just send 'em over or I'll take my trade elsewhere!"

A half hour later the three trollops arrived ready for business. They seemed rather puzzled, on being ushered in, to find Alex there alone. Looking around, one of the girls said, "Where are the other two fellas?"

"There are no others," said Alex, a mysterious look on his face. "There's no one here but little me."

"I'll bite," said another girl. "What's the gimmick?"

"There is no gimmick." Alex smiled.

"Well, then, what're ya going to do with the three of us that ya couldn't do with just one or two?" She took a closer look at him. "With just one?"

"I'm not going to do anything with any of you. Just sit down at that table over there, take off your shoes and relax," he said.

"Just our shoes? Boy! This is some party!"

Another girl piped up, "What's the matter, Alex, do we look that beat up?"

"Not at all, girls," he reassured them. "You look just great. Now then, I assume you know how to play poker?"

Rather puzzled, the first girl said, "Oh, sure, we play it a lot when business is slack."

Alex got out two bottles of booze, two decks of cards and several packs of cigarettes. For the next five hours they played poker. He deliberately misplayed every hand. He wanted the girls to win, and they did. Besides that, he paid them their standard price for a night of love.

At three in the morning Alex laid down the cards, leaned back in his chair and said, "That's it girls. I'm tired and I'm going to hit the sack."

Women are strange creatures. Financially they had had a very successful evening, but all three were rather hurt that all he wanted from them was an evening of cards.

Alex is now fifty-three. He is married and has two grown children. Any night he can bribe the kids to stay home, the four of them play poker. No money changes hands. The air is clean and so are the jokes. Although it's fun, it's not the fun it used to be. But then, when you're fifty-three, what is?

3

Chico's Bank Account

 Chico was the gambler of the Marx Brothers. He didn't care anything about money except that he knew without it he couldn't gamble, and if he couldn't gamble life was just a bowl of sawdust. He was a great card player. Perhaps one of the greatest. Compared with the contributions made by Einstein, Beethoven, and Salk, I admit this wasn't much of a distinction, but then, "one man's meat, etc."

He bet against the Yankees for fifteen years. I don't mean in the Civil War, I mean in the American League. He once said, "There's no point in betting on the Yankees. They're almost certain to win. Give me the long shots every time!"

So, at the end of each season, Chico would be in about the same financial position he was in at the beginning, only a little worse. His spirits flourished on the turn of a card, the spin of the wheel and the galloping nags, and if there was no other action around he would pitch pennies for dollars. If he was real desperate he would even pitch dollars for pennies. Someone once asked him how much money he had lost over the years. He said, "Find out how much Harpo has. That's how much I've lost!"

This constant struggle to make a buck the easy way made it imperative for him to work during the off season. While the rest of us were living high off the hog, Chico was living off the other end. He had to keep working to ward off his creditors, although it was an exciting life, it was an extremely arduous one.

One summer, heavily in debt, he contracted to play a group of night clubs in several large Southern cities. I won't mention the name of the first city or its mayor. For all I know this mayor may still be running the town. He had come to this country from Italy as a small boy, and by hard work and a few crooked deals, he became the head of one of the liveliest cities in the South before he was forty. Although his salary was only $15,000 a year, he was enormously wealthy. It wasn't easy to get rich on the pin money the city paid him, what with taxes and everything, but he had a talent for investing his money in the right places.

Chico always played an Italian immigrant on the stage, and his characterization was so authentic that most people couldn't understand how he could possibly be my brother. Too frequently I was confronted with this question, "How can Chico be your brother when he's Italian and you're Jewish?" I finally grew weary of answering this riddle and told them that if it bothered them that much, go take it up with my mother and father. To the best of my knowledge, Chico was my brother, and the only reason he essayed the role of an immigrant Italian was because it happened to lend itself to his particular comedic talents. When that explanation didn't satisfy people, I told them to take it up with the Department of Immigration, and if they got no satisfaction there to try the Department of Agriculture.

The mayor was a hot sport. He loved the night life. Since this thriving metropolis happened to be his home town, it was naturally wide open.

The first night Chico opened at this night club, the mayor was spread out at a front table. He loved Chico's piano playing, but most of all he loved the way he spoke. It reminded him of his native Naples. He could almost hear the mandolins tinkling in the barber shops and smell the strings of garlic swaying in the breeze and adding pungency to it. He was proud of Chico; he was proud of himself; and he was proud of all the money he was able to steal from the people. He was proud that Chico, a famous comedian, was an Italian, a lovable countryman who had sprung from the same soil as he.

As soon as the opening performance was over, the mayor rushed backstage, threw his arms around Chico and kissed him on both cheeks. For the next two weeks he was there every night. He and Chico became very friendly. He loved Chico and Chico was very fond of the mayor. They were together all day. At night, after the show, they would go out on the town. But Chico never told the mayor that he was born in Yorkville in New York City, a neighborhood that was not only not Italian but almost a hundred per cent German.

On the last night of the engagement, the mayor, as usual, went backstage to the dressing room. To his dismay, he saw Chico packing.

"Chico!" he cried, "whatsamatter? Why you pack up

your clothes? You no like it here? Why you want to leave for?"

Chico explained that he was opening the following night in Birmingham, Alabama.

"Birmingham is a lousy town," declared the mayor. "Why you don't stay here? This here is the best town inna whole South!"

"Now look," said Chico, "I like you very much and I also like the town, but I can't stay here. I'm in show business. That's how I make my living. And tomorrow I open in Birmingham."

The mayor threw his arms around Chico. "Chico," he pleaded, "you're Italian, I'm Italian. I got no children. Not-a one bambino." (He neglected to say he'd never been married.) In his grief he then reverted to his mother tongue

and let loose a steady stream of Italian histrionics. Chico just stood there, hoping that a word would seep through that he would recognize. In fact, he almost forgot himself and started to answer in German.

"Chico, my boy," the mayor continued, fortunately reverting to English, "you stay here. You quit show business. You jus' stay here with me an' I fix you up good."

"How?" asked Chico.

The mayor pinched Chico's cheek. "Look," he said in a low voice, "I own twenty sporting houses in this here town. All ten-dollar ones, too. You stay here with me an' you know what I do? I give you five-a these houses, all for you'-self. You never gotta do a day's work again if you live to be a hundred!"

Chico later told me he was tempted and almost said, "Make it eight houses and I'll stay." But, he said, the call of the theater was stronger than the call of the mayor and all his wenches. As he gypsied all over the country, following the action, there was always the thought in the back of his mind that if things got too tough he could always retire to his li'l ole plantation houses in the South, where there would always be a red light burning in the window just for him.

4

A Hot Time in the Cold Town Tonight

There was once an American named Larry Blank who was an extremely talented comedian but could never quite make it in his own country. So, being no fool, he decided to pull up stakes and seek greener pastures. His particular green field turned out to be London. For some reason or other the British thought he was the funniest comedian since Henry VIII, and almost overnight he became a star.

He earned a big salary being funny, but his biggest source of income was gambling. There was hardly anything he couldn't do with a deck of cards, and there was hardly anything he didn't do. His specialties were poker and auction pinochle, and to be sure no one would win any of his money he had devised a very simple solution. He marked the cards. He did this so skillfully that the indentations on the deck could only be seen if one came to the game equipped with an oversized magnifying glass. Luckily for him, very few card players travel around with this sort of equipment.

Between his theatrical career and his gambling, he was probably the richest actor in England. But he was a miserly ham and lived in a rather shabby flat in Soho.

We were appearing in London at the time, and Chico and Harpo, who were both pretty handy with a deck (the fact is, they were two of the best card players in the States) began playing poker with Mr. Blank.

Mr. Blank's reputation as a card shark had preceded him. No one accused him of being dishonest, but on the other hand no one accused him of being honest. The consensus among his slim coterie of friends, most of whom had been victimized playing cards with him, was that there was not only something rotten in Denmark but there was something pretty fishy going on in Soho.

It wasn't until Harpo and Chico lost two weeks' salary inside of a week that they came to the conclusion that Mr. Blank's success at the poker table could not be attributed entirely to luck. He won too steadily and in too curious a manner for this. Chico and Harpo finally realized that they were being taken, and concluded that if they expected to sail back to the States in any class above that of stowaway they had better do a little fleecing of their own. One day they casually remarked to this card dazzler, "You're too lucky at poker. Let's play auction pinochle next time."

Mr. Blank didn't mind. Marked cards were marked cards. As long as he had an edge, he was willing to play anything they suggested from Fan-Tan to Old Maid.

The bidding in auction pinochle is somewhat similar to that in bridge, and it was a simple matter for the boys to set up a series of signals telling each other what cards they were holding and how each one was to bid. The following night, as they sat down to play, Mr. Blank whipped out two decks of cards and said, "Let's go."

Chico said, "If you don't mind, Larry, we've brought along a couple of brand-new decks with the seals unbroken. You see, I have an allergy that I picked up in the Orient and I always start sneezing when I smell old cards."

Mr. Blank realized that they had spiked some of his guns but he was confident that with his card sense he could trim these suckers even without a marked deck. "Fine," he said rather briskly. "Sorry about your allergy. I played in Hong Kong once and it certainly stinks." After this brief travelogue he said, "Okay, let's get started."

Mr. Blank's room was the last word in discomfort. It contained four chairs, a table, and a tiny fireplace where four miniature logs burned faintly in the foreground. If you are familiar with the discomforts of a cold-water flat in Soho it may help you to understand why the British Empire has steadily declined over the years.

From midnight to 3 A.M. Mr. Blank lost steadily, and by a strange coincidence Chico and Harpo won steadily. Within three hours they had collected quite a wad of Mr. Blank's money and were ready to quit. Mr. Blank, however, unaccustomed to losing, was desperate and pleaded with them to continue. They said they would love to go on, but pointed out that although the temperature in the flat was fine for ice skating it hardly lent itself to indoor games.

Finally they agreed to continue on one condition. Mr. Blank would have to dig up some more logs for the fire. But Mr. Blank said, "It's three o'clock in the morning. I can't get any logs at this hour."

The boys, way ahead and eager to leave, said, "Sorry, in that case the game is over."

"Look, fellows," he said, "the furniture in this room is all second-hand stuff. I bought it years ago for practically nothing. Would you continue playing if I broke up one of these chairs for fuel?"

It was rather a plaintive speech. Chico and Harpo, both with hearts of gold, were almost in tears.

"Fine," they answered. They knew they had him hooked, and they knew that the longer they played the more of Mr. Blank's money would change hands.

It was a hungry, enthusiastic fire. In no time at all, the chair was consumed. Again the room grew cold. Then a second chair was thrown into the flames. The boys were still winning; comforted by the unusual warmth and the large sum they were extracting from Mr. Blank's bankroll, they were downright happy. Finally, however, the last chair went up the chimney.

They were now playing on their knees. Had someone entered the room at this point and not noticed the cards, he might have assumed from this tableau that here were three deeply religious Mohammedans facing the East and praying to Mecca.

Now that the fire had gone out, the temperature again began slipping down toward the South Pole. Our tricky friend was desperate. He couldn't understand why he was losing so steadily. It had never happened to him before. Had they done something to the cards that even he couldn't detect? No, it couldn't be. He had seen them open the new decks right before his eyes. If he could only keep them there a while longer he was sure that his luck would change and he would win all his money back. He pleaded with the boys rather pathetically, "Won't you play just one more hour?"

"We'd like to, Larry," said Harpo, "but look at my

fingers. They're blue and numb. I can hardly deal the cards."

Chico said, "The other day I read in the papers that the dread ice age which has been predicted for centuries is coming pretty soon. I think it arrived tonight."

Mr. Blank threw them a wan smile and said, "I know this sounds crazy, but if I chopped up the table and threw it in the grate would you consider sitting on the floor and continuing the game on the carpet? It's a cheap table and it never did match the rest of the furniture."

Since the rest of the furniture had already gone up the flue, this didn't make much sense, but my guess is that by

this time his brain had addled from this unaccustomed blow to his fortunes and his mind had become partly unhinged.

The boys, still winning, said, "Okay. As a matter of fact, we prefer playing on the floor."

Chunk by chunk, the table was fed to the fire. When its carcass, too, had been sacrificed to the flames, the cold again returned like a poor relative on Christmas Eve. Harpo started sneezing and Chico's teeth were chattering. Chico finally said, "Well, Larry, it's seven o'clock. We're freezing and we're hungry. We're going back to the hotel to thaw out and get some food."

Mr. Blank, incidentally, in addition to being a crook, was not noted as the most gracious host in London. The boys had been there seven hours and the only nourishment he had given them was a cup of Bovril and some crackers.

By seven o'clock of a cold, rainy, foggy morning, Mr. Blank was out six thousand dollars and a complete set of furniture, and the boys were in six thousand dollars and were flirting with pneumonia and malnutrition. The game had to stop. It was their lives against his money. There was nothing left to throw into the fireplace. For if the truth must be known, even the fat was in the fire. Mr. Blank, frantic, his back against the wall, finally toyed with the idea of throwing himself into the fireplace, but after thinking it over decided against it. How could he play pinochle if he was on fire? So Mr. Blank, for the first time in a long and crooked career, was forced to call it a losing night.

Before leaving, Chico and Harpo handed Mr. Blank twenty dollars and suggested he buy a cord of wood in case they played there again. He was a crook but he was no fool. He took the twenty and said, "I don't think we'll play again. I've had it—and I think I've been had!"

Out on the landing, Harpo and Chico shook hands glee-
fully with each other, stumbled down the dark, dank stair-
case, hailed a cab and instructed the driver to take them
as quickly as possible to the warmest restaurant in London.
The driver seemed rather puzzled at this request. "I say,"
he said, "don't you want a *good* restaurant?"

"We don't care if it's good or not," said Harpo. "Just
take us where it's warm. After our blood starts circulating
again we'll decide where to eat."

5

Rats in the Cat House

There is no point in mentioning the town or the actor. He usually appeared in the legitimate theater, but the play he had appeared in flopped and so he condescended to play a few vaudeville dates, winding up on the bill with my brothers and me. He was tall, handsome, and dressed and looked like what he was—a big, dumb, stuffy ham.

He had been invited, along with us, to one of the fanciest sporting houses in the city. Although we weren't crazy about his company, we didn't voice any objections to his joining us.

Like most egomaniacs, he was utterly humorless. But what he lacked in humor he made up in offensiveness. We were no sooner seated in the parlor than he began aiming a steady barrage of unfunny ribaldry at the girls and the madam.

If they liked you in these houses, they loved you. If they didn't like you, the best thing to do was to clear out before you were deep in trouble. You could get your skull accidentally crushed by a beer bottle, you could have your wallet lifted, and if you got too far out of line the madam would summon the bouncer who was an expert at tossing unwanted guests out on their *derrières*.

We arrived about eleven-thirty, sang a few songs, and had a beer and some sandwiches. At about one we started to say good-by, when the madam came over to our friend, the legit, and in her most gracious manner invited him to spend the night. With his customary tact he immediately asked how much this would cost. The madam, in her sweetest voice, replied, "Not a nickel to you, honey. All the girls are crazy about you. You're all they've been talking about the whole evening. They pleaded with me to invite you to stay all night as a guest."

The following day, just before the matinee, Shakespeare walked into our dressing room. His face was whiter than many of the sheets I've slept on. He then proceeded to tell us how he had fared the night before.

After we had gone, he said, the prettiest girl in the place came over to him. She said that the madam had held a lottery among the girls and she had been the lucky one who was going to have the pleasure of his company for the entire night. "Honey," she whispered, "you go upstairs to the last room down the hall and get undressed. I'll be up in just a few minutes, honey." (Honey was the standard term of endearment in those places.)

"Well, I found the room at the end of the hall," he continued. "I opened the door and went inside. I looked around and was a little puzzled by the absence of furniture. Except for a frayed army cot in one corner, the room was absolutely bare. No carpet, no chairs, no dresser. Suddenly I heard a key turn in the lock. I quickly went to the door and tried it. It didn't open. 'This is some kind of a gag,' I said to myself, 'but I'll go along with it. I know that girl is crazy about me. She told me so. In a few minutes I'm sure she'll open this door and probably usher me into a beautiful bedroom.'

"It was fairly dark in the room, with only one small bulb hanging from the ceiling. 'Well,' I thought, 'there's no point in just standing here. I'll get undressed as she told me to, and then lie down on the cot.' Since there was no closet in the room, I carefully folded my clothes and placed them on the floor. I kept staring at the door, expecting it to open at any moment.

"Presently I heard a strange squeaking noise coming from the far side of the room. In the gloom I spied a large rat emerging from a hole in the baseboard. I ran to the door, hammered on it and then began to shout, 'Let me out! Open the door!' But nobody answered. I went back and sat on the edge of the cot. I must admit I was shaking a bit. The squeaking continued and I picked up a shoe and hurled it at the rat. He was too fast for me, though, and I didn't get him. To my relief, he disappeared. I started to lie down again, and again I heard the squeaking noises. This time I took careful aim and threw the other shoe. In the next fifteen minutes I had thrown all my clothes over there, and now rats began to appear from half a dozen places in the room."

He shuddered. "I was panicky by this time. You know, rats have always frightened me. I think I would rather face a lion than a rat!

"I ran to the door and started screaming, 'Let me out! Let me out, do you hear me? Let me out of here!' I then

twisted the knob desperately and, to my surprise, it was open! Evidently while I was screaming somebody had crept up and unlocked it.

"Shouting at the rats to scare them away, I ran over to the far wall, frantically gathered my clothing and shoes, stood on the cot and quickly dressed myself. I then flew to the door, ran down the stairs and out into the street. As I stood there on the sidewalk, still shaking, I heard sounds of laughter. I looked up. In an open window on the second floor I spotted the madam and her six girls, all laughing hysterically.

"I ran all the way back to the hotel, rushed up to my room, locked the door and quickly swallowed five sleeping pills. I finally managed to doze off!"

Even though we didn't like him, I must admit we felt sorry for the ham as he concluded his macabre story. I have rarely seen a man so shaken.

After a few minutes he pulled himself together, left our dressing room and notified the manager that in his present condition he would be unable to appear in the Shakespearean vignette he had been performing for the peasants. Later that evening he took the train back to New York.

I don't know how the madam and her girls did it, but you'll have to admit it was a hell of a trick, rounding up all those rats in a cat house.

6

The Prepaid Lover

 The head of one of the big New York advertising agencies was a tall, humorless Pennsylvania Dutchman with the average number of wives and children and the usual fancy offices on Madison Avenue and in Hollywood.

Every other month or so, business took him on a flying visit to the West Coast office. He looked forward to these trips with great anticipation, for although he loved his wife, he regarded himself as quite a ladies' man. And California, to him, was the happy hunting ground.

Since he was a power in television, he was invited to most of the big parties; but these, he soon discovered, weren't much fun. Most of the girls were either married or spoken for.

Sometimes he would date one of the secretaries in his office, but he was about sixty and hardly a barrel of laughs. Soon, most of the girls began ducking his invitations. It quickly got around that, although he dined them well, the next step invariably was an invitation to accompany him to his hotel suite.

One of the television performers working for this agency was none too certain that his option would be picked up for the following season; he knew, however, that our friend, Mr. Fred Schultz, was all-powerful, and if he said the word you were sure to be renewed for the next year.

For purposes of no identification, let's call this performer Joe Cool. One day Joe phoned Mr. Schultz. "Freddie, boy," he began, "this is your old friend, Joe Cool. I heard from my agent that you just blew into town and I know how lonely you are when you're away from home. Well, have I got a girl for you!"

Mr. Schultz said, "Joe, I'm going to tell you something I've never told anyone before and I hope you won't repeat it to anyone else, especially my wife." He laughed heartily at this. For a stern businessman this seemed like a pretty funny joke—to him.

Joe Cool, thinking of next season's option, joined in the laughter. "Fred, you sure get off some hot ones! If you'd-a gone into show business, you'd-a been one heluva comic!"

"Joe," Schultz continued, "I'm going to be frank and give you this straight from the shoulder. It's true, I've taken out a lot of girls in this town. I'm ashamed to say it, but I never seem to get anywhere with them. To be blunt about it, I never score. Oh sure, they go out to dinner with me, or to a movie or a preview, but when it comes to getting down to cases—you know what I mean—they usually say 'Not tonight, I've got a sick headache,' or 'I've got to get up early in the morning.'

"Now you know I'm not any gay Lothario. I realize I

just hit sixty and I've got a little pot belly, but I've still got all my own teeth and I'm as strong as an ox. Yet all I ever get is a fast kiss and a 'Thank you, Mr. Schultz, for a lovely evening.' The only one I'm successful in getting into the hay is my wife, and after thirty years of marriage that's about as exciting as seeing a third rerun of *Wagon Train.*"

"Freddie, boy," Joe said, "your problems are over. I got something lined up for you that'll make your ears flap!" He could almost see Mr. Schultz' smile over the phone.

"Joe, you're a sweetheart!" Schultz boomed. The dejection left his voice and he sounded as pepped up as though he had just swallowed two benzedrine tablets.

"How would you like to meet a twenty-two-year-old blonde with measurements like—ah, what's the use of going through all this? She's got a shape like Jayne Mansfield and she's single. You throw three Martinis into her and she'll climb up the bedroom wall! And don't go gettin' the idea that she's some kinda tramp. She's a very nice girl, but she's lonely."

Mr. Schultz was so excited over this brief description that he was becoming incoherent. It ceased to be a conversation. "Who is she?" he panted. "Where is she—and how soon can we get together?"

"Fred, I got it all laid out for you," said Joe. (I hope you readers will pardon the accidental vulgarity.) "She'll knock on your hotel door at 7:30 this evening. And don't worry because you don't look so hot. She likes mature men."

It was then five o'clock. Schultz rushed to his hotel and immediately phoned room service. He ordered a quart of vodka, gin, bourbon, Scotch, brandy, Irish whisky, assorted cordials, White Rock, Ginger Ale, Seven-Up and ice. He was taking no chances.

After the booze arrived he still had an hour to wait, so he phoned his wife in Pennsylvania and told her how much he missed her. "Darling, I can't tell you how unhappy I am when I'm away from you," he lied. At home he didn't always talk this way. Sometimes he didn't talk to her at all. But now his conscience was troubling him, and his wife was so pleased with his call that she gave each of the children an extra helping of Philadelphia scrapple.

At 7:30 there came a dainty knock on the door. As the girl entered, he bowed low. So low that he got a severe twitch in his sacroiliac. Despite this, he straightened up and greeted her warmly. He was so grateful to get a dame up to his room who looked like the real thing that he even kissed her hand. He was beginning to feel like Charles Boyer already.

As they drank he eyed her luscious assets with all the intensity of a cobra eyeing a fat chicken or a small boy looking into the window of a candy store. He ordered dinner for two. After the meal had been consumed and the dishes and waiter removed, there was some scattered, desultory conversation. Then, carefully picking his words, he timidly suggested that they hit the sack.

In less than one minute flat she stood before him in her birthday suit. Apparently she didn't have much on when she arrived, but from the speed with which she stripped, Mr. Schultz later observed that, had she been a man, she would have made a heluva fireman.

I abhor obscenity and vulgarity so I will spare the reader the sordid details. Suffice it to say (as my attorney always puts it), that this dainty, demure, little girl showed him some tricks in the course of a wonderful night which he would have bet were not even possible.

After breakfast he told her he had to go to the office and hoped he would see her again. Rather hesitantly, before saying good-by, he mentioned money.

"Mr. Schultz," she protested, "I didn't spend the night with you for money. I'm not that kind of a girl. You see, I had heard about you and I knew that if we ever met I would like you a lot. I've always been nuts about businessmen."

Delighted at this compliment, he kissed her passionately, exhausted though he was from her spectacular performance the night before. He was a proud man.

When he arrived at the office he told the Chairman of the Board and a few of the Vice-Presidents about his experience. He even boasted about how good he was. "You know," he said, "in the last few years I had an idea that a beautiful young girl wouldn't be attracted to me, but last night I realized that I'm still a pretty good man."

Of course, what he didn't know was that this innocent, lovely creature was a fairly well-known prostitute around town who had been engaged by Joe Cool to spend the night with Mr. Schultz for a hundred dollars net.

There is no point in repeating the details, but every time Mr. Schultz came to Hollywood, Joe Cool had another tramp lined up for him. In the course of a few years it probably cost him several thousand dollars. It's true that he couldn't write this off on his income tax, but on the other hand Joe's option was picked up every season.

It was a wonderful arrangement for all concerned, including the wife in Pennsylvania. She was happy, too, for she just loved making scrapple for the children.

7

La Leçon Française

There is a producer in this town who averages about seven thousand dollars a week, and if you are any good with figures you know this puts him in the ninety per cent tax bracket. He married a girl out of Woolworth's. I don't mean to imply that she was worth only ten cents. The fact of the matter is, she's a very pretty wench. They settled down in a beautiful home with two expensive cars, two expensive children, and all the luxuries that money could buy.

During the first two years she was a happy housewife. She didn't have to scrub the floors or wash the diapers. She graced the head of the table, and if there were any guests, she listened attentively to all the theatrical talk being tossed around.

Now there is, indeed, no business like show business. There is hardly a man or woman alive who doesn't crave exposure on the stage, screen, or rostrum. The world is full of exhibitionists. I think most people enter politics so that they can climb up on a platform and let other people look at them. This is why the quiz and panel shows were such a success. Thousands of people wrote to the networks, begging for a chance to appear on these shows. In most cases it wasn't the money that interested them. They just wanted to appear before an audience. As an obscure poet named Shakespeare so aptly put it, "All the world's a stage," and it seems as though everyone wants to be on it, front and center.

Well, this producer's wife was no exception. As happens to all females, she was bit by the bug. One day she informed her husband that she wanted to go into show business. He pointed out that there were eighteen thousand young, attractive girls in Hollywood who also wanted to crash show business and who were also out of work.

"That's probably true," she agreed, "but they're not married to you. Don't forget, you're an important man in the movie industry and I'm sure you can open many doors for me."

"I don't know what doors you're referring to," he said, "but why do you have to be in show business? Why don't you take up painting or music or even learn a foreign language or two? A little culture wouldn't do you any harm."

"Oh, those things all bore me," she shrugged. "I just know I've got it in me to be a great actress and neither you nor anyone else can stop me!"

This wasn't quite the attitude she had when he pulled her out of the ten-cent store, but marriage and thoughts of alimony do strange things to women.

"Get me any kind of a part," she insisted. "I don't care how small it is. Once they see me on film I'll bet you next month's allowance (which, incidentally, she had already spent) that I'll be deluged with offers."

The producer had a lot of friends, and one day he came home and told her that he almost got her a part in a picture. It was only two lines but, unfortunately, they needed a girl who could say them in French.

"What kind of a part is it?" she asked excitedly. "Is it anything like the role Elizabeth Taylor had in *Cat on a Hot Tin Roof?*"

"Well, not exactly," he said. "It's a scene in the United Nations and all the delegates, male and female, from all over the world are assembled."

She was ecstatic. "Suppose I could learn to say the lines in French. Would I get the part?"

"I guess so. But, remember, it's just two lines."

Although she didn't need the money, her next question was, "How much will they pay me?"

"Since it's a speaking part, you would get two hundred dollars for the one day's shooting," her husband said.

"Wonderful! I'll take it!" And off she went to phone the news to all her friends.

The next day she appeared at the local Berlitz office where she quickly signed up for a series of one hundred French lessons for one thousand dollars. This done, she trotted off to the record shop where she bought a dozen French recordings and then to the book store where, in short order, they unloaded upon her the works of Sartre, Anatole France, and Balzac, all in the original.

The picture wasn't due to start for two months, and by that time she was proficient enough to order a complete meal in a French resturant. Finally came the day of her big scene. She rattled off the two lines in French with all the authority of De Gaulle telling the Algerians to get the hell out of Paris.

When she received her salary check she found that, what with deductions for withholding, state unemployment insurance, disability insurance, and the Motion Picture Relief Fund, all that was left was $142. Her husband who, as I've already mentioned, was in the ninety per cent tax bracket, had to pay the income tax on the gross amount of $200, plus the thousand for the French lessons. After paying for the books and the records herself, she netted twenty dollars. He, on the other hand, was out almost twelve hundred.

When the picture was previewed they discovered it was forty minutes too long, so the scene in the United Nations was completely eliminated.

She has now taken up Yoga.

The moral to this episode is: if you have to buy something, go to Saks Fifth Avenue, not to Woolworth's. A ten-cent purchase can be awfully expensive.

8

One for and on the Road

 Now that we've come almost to the end of this section of this monumental tome, don't say "Thank God!"—because I still have a little way to go. Be patient. Remember, I'm just as confused by all this as you are. Confuseder!

No one has ever been able to put the definitive finger on sex. It's an intangible that has mystified and baffled every scientist, philosopher, and urologist since the days when Aphrodite scampered through the woods in her didies. Incidentally, for what it's worth, there were all kinds of Aphrodites scattered throughout the Grecian and Roman Empires. For example, the one in Sicily was half-man and half-woman. Sometimes, on a dull day when there was no one of either sex to play with, Aphrodite would go chase herself. This is how the expression, "Go chase yourself!" originated.

To resume, Henry VIII, sometimes known as Old Pot-

155

Belly, obviously didn't know his stomach from his nether regions, for he was once heard to remark that the way to a man's heart was through his stomach. This may have been true during the days when England ruled the waves and Henry used to knock off a leg of boar (and an occasional wife) for breakfast, but today you'll notice that no one who's anybody gets married in a delicatessen.

I don't deny that a well-fed, normal, nonulcerous stomach may be a factor in the pursuit of love, but perhaps I had better begin at the beginning.

Many years ago, while slumming in the dregs of small-time vaudeville, we were stabled in a boarding house in a way station called Orange, Texas. In addition to the four Marx Brothers, this shabby ménage consisted of six Mexican railroad laborers, a Mexican landlady, and her Mexican daughter. In fiction we have always been led to believe that the daughter of a farmer or a boarding house keeper was invariably an irresistible knockout. Well, this daughter, Pepita by name, was unfortunately a dog. Her exterior assets comprised a set of crooked teeth, a slanting bust, and a nose that resembled a relief map of the upper Andes.

Although we were very young, always on the scent, and not too choosey, Pepita was a challenge to which no sane man would care to respond.

When we checked into the boarding house we had no idea that the cuisine was going to be lower Rio Grande; therefore we were a littled puzzled the first morning to discover that breakfast was a simple meal of hot tamales and Mexican coffee. If you've never swallowed this brand of coffee, I can describe it in a few words. It was chicory with a dash of ground mud. It wasn't something you could drink.

It had to be vigorously chewed before it would stop chewing back and surrender.

Tamales for breakfast struck us as a peculiar substitute for eggs. And we certainly weren't accustomed to frijoles for lunch. But that night, when the landlady served her *pièce de résistance,* hot chili con carne, we knew that although we were not in Mexico our stomachs were bulging in that direction.

The three meals didn't set too well, and we spent most of the night groaning, tossing, and turning. Tuesday's and Wednesday's bill of fare was the same as Monday's. It didn't vary by one chili bean. By Wednesday night we had eaten so much of this peppery swill that most of our time between meals was occupied in consuming frequent draughts of water in a vain effort to quench the fires blazing within us.

After nine Mexican meals in three days, we realized that water in customary quantities was not the answer to our problem. What we needed was a strong, steady stream. A fire hose could have done the trick, but unfortunately there was none available—not even at the fire house.

The Mexican laborers lapped up the food as though it were edible—and clamored for more. We ate it. We didn't want it, but it was either that or a CARE package. And in those days the CARE package had not yet been invented.

That night, on the way to our room, Harpo, under the delusion that jumping up and down might help dispose of the fiery fodder, began doing his conception of "The Cucaracha."

Our bedroom contained two beds, a bowl, a pitcher, and a tiny towel for each victim. Since running water hadn't as yet penetrated this section of Texas, the water in the pitcher quickly disappeared. Though it was in the dead of winter, the room required no heat. Our four stomachs, loaded with chili peppers, Tabasco, and red beans, exuded enough warmth to heat not only our room but the entire boarding house. My guess is that between us, we could have kept Madison Square Garden warm on the coldest night of the year.

By Wednesday night, the cumulative effect of this Latin diet was beginning to take its toll. We hardly slept at all through the concert of rumbles, gurgles, extraneous cursing, and other animal sounds that echoed through the room.

We were reluctant to get up on Thursday morning and face another day of Mexican fodder. We would have eaten at a lunch wagon but we had no cash. In those days all actors, especially in boarding houses, were suspect and were obliged to pay in advance. The alternatives were three more days of this grub or starvation.

That morning, four desperate youths held a council of war. Since I was the only one with a mustache, I took the floor.

"Boys," I began, "I think we are willing to concede that we are jolly good fellows and love life. Right?" The boys nodded their heads in unison. "Now then, I've got an idea so brilliant that it doesn't seem possible that I thought it up. If it works, our last three days here won't be our last three days, if you get what I mean. Listen carefully. We have all seen and avoided Pepita, the landlady's repulsive daughter. Now then, it is not our custom as actors and Marx Brothers to ignore any young woman unless she is sub-human, but if we want to remain alive one of us is going to have to make the supreme sacrifice. To put it bluntly, one of us is going to have to spend a night with Pepita. He's going to have to tell her he's madly in love with her and

that the only thing keeping them apart is this alien menu. It's going to be his task to make Pepita persuade her mother to feed us American food for the balance of the week. As he fondles her gently, he is to whisper in one of her over-sized ears that he can't live without her, but her mother's victuals are raising hell with his and his brothers' entrails. As he holds her in his arms he is to promise her that if she can swing this for us he, in return, will do for her what no man has ever done for a woman since the Garden of Eden."

Sick as we all were from the food, the thought of an affair with Pepita made us even sicker. At this point, Harpo, still under the delusion that shaking himself violently would alleviate the burning pains in his alimentary canal, began doing "The Cucaracha."

"Now, gentlemen—or brothers, if you prefer," I continued, "we all know that it is traditional in the armed forces, when there is a particularly hazardous duty to be performed, to issue a call for volunteers. Since we are, fortunately, not in the army, although it would certainly be an improvement over this dump, it is obvious after seeing Pepita that no one is going to volunteer. Do I see a show of hands? I thought not! Therefore, since we are all men of high honor, I suggest we draw straws. The lucky one, if you will permit a horse-laugh at this point, will have the pleasure of spending a whole night doing what comes unnaturally with this young monster. I ask you, who could ask for anything more?"

There were several ribald answers to this question, none of which I care to go into now. Remember, this book has to go through the mail.

"To put it succinctly," I went on, "tonight's lucky lover will not only rescue his brothers and, incidentally, himself, from ptomaine poisoning, but he will experience a night of love that I dare say he will remember to his dying day!"

As soon as the moaning subsided, I quickly produced four matchsticks and began praying silently that I would be spared.

I am too kind to mention the name of the unfortunate brother whom fate decided to punish. The survivors, delirious with joy at having escaped physical contact with the fair Pepita, were quick to offer advice and encouragement. The condemned man wept briefly, but it did him little good, for he knew there was no way out. Had he tried to reneg, the three more fortunate ones would have flogged him to a jelly.

At the breakfast table Thursday morning, while gagging on a large plate of tamales, the loser of the draw (let's call him Brother X) began his campaign by throwing sheep's eyes and loving glances at the Mexican maiden.

To say that she was surprised and flattered is putting it mildly. In a house bulging with ten passionate men, this was the first time any male had ever looked at her with anything but nausea. Being a woman, she quickly took the bait. She began flashing her beady eyes at him and smiling through her jagged teeth.

The flirting and amorous exchanges continued all through lunch. After the inevitable chili that evening, Pepita was his captive. As he left for the theater, Brother X asked her, with a shudder, if she would care to meet him after the performance. Later that night, as they sat in the swing in the back yard, she told him that if there was anything he wanted, all he had to do was mention it. "But first, my beautiful señor," she cooed, "I long to be seen in your arms."

Appalled as he was at this suggestion, Brother X was no coward. "Listen, my Mexican rose," he said, "later tonight you can have all of me"—he neglected to mention that after four days of Mexican grub there was damned little left of him—"but first I must tell you something. As you know, my brothers and I adore the Mexican people. We love your ways and customs and we have always admired your country's struggle for independence. But your mother's food, although it compares favorably with some of the great restaurants in the East, unfortunately is not the food we're accustomed to and it's left our stomachs and libidos almost beyond repair."

"*Amor mio*," she purred, "I am so sorry our food does not agree weeth you." (This was the understatement of the week!) "But anything you weesh to eat, my mamma weel feex for you. Kees me, *corazón*. I love you." As she moved toward him, he instinctively backed away.

"My dear Pepita," he said, with one foot out of the swing, "all we want from your lovely mother who, by the way, is almost as glamorous as you are, is eggs, fried chicken, a chop or two, and the basic staples of the country-side."

And so, gentle reader, let us draw the curtain on what promises to be the most lopsided affair since David fought Goliath.

To quote John Milton (1608–1674), " 'Tis chastity, my brother, chastity. She that has that is clad in complete steel." Well, you would certainly have to say that about Pepita.

Friday morning dawned clear. Not a cloud was in the sky. A faint westerly wind caressed the horizon and, incidentally, swept the delicious aroma of bacon and eggs into the dining room.

I still won't mention the name of the brother who spent most of the previous night with the ugly duckling, but he must have been mighty effective in the clinches! For lunch we had fried chicken and hot biscuits. Dinner that evening was a parade of T-bone steaks, baked potatoes, and watermelon topped off with huge scoops of ice cream.

The other three vainly questioned the martyred brother about the previous night. The usual gamey remarks were thrown at him—the kind of crude, stale vulgarities that are invariably tossed at the unfortunate groom at a bachelor party. But Brother X, like all great men who have given their all, refused to talk. He just smiled wanly.

Pepita, on the other hand, was full of bounce and ginger and flirted outrageously with her lover all through the three meals. Whenever she looked at him, he looked the other way. When she served the food, she rubbed against the table, trying vainly to experience once more the thrill of his body. But he was no fool. The closer she came, the farther he pulled his chair away from the table, prepared, if necessary, to run or dive under it.

As soon as the last spoonful of ice cream had been consumed, Brother X, ignoring Pepita's appealing glances and aggressive advances, fled from the dining room and ran all the way to the theater. In the dressing room, his brothers showered him with praise. The boys, their stomachs freed from four days of Mexican hog wash, gave a magnificent performance. All through the show they kept slapping their hero on the back and congratulating him. I must say, this mystified the audience, but our act usually mystified the audience anyway, so this was no concern of ours.

After the performance, we returned to the boarding house. There was Pepita, hungry for another night of ecstasy, sitting by the front door sniffing a rose and waiting for her lover.

Our hero was alert. Spying his personal gargoyle sitting there, he quickly sneaked around to the back of the house, climbed in through an open window, ran up to the room and securely locked the door. We had a tough time convincing him we were not Pepita.

We slept well and quietly that night. Saturday morning, our last day, rolled around (as it always does after Friday). We licked our chops in anticipation of those three more delectable meals waiting for us. Hurriedly dressing, we trooped down for breakfast.

The realization that hell hath no fury like a woman scorned didn't occur to us until Pepita appeared and slapped a large dish of tamales on the table. For lunch we had frijoles. And for dinner? You're right. Chili con carne and Mexican coffee.

So you see, despite Henry VIII, the way to a man's heart is not necessarily through his stomach. In this case the way to our stomachs was through Brother X's heart.

And I ought to know, for I was Brother X.

Part Five

Marxist Philosophy, According to Groucho

1

What This Country Really Needs

I want to say at the outset that I am not a candidate for anything. I just like to sound off. The Marx-for-Vice-President boom never had my support, nor did it ever get very far. It was launched by an obscure Californian who was politically inexperienced and, incidentally, very drunk.

The whole thing was nothing if not spontaneous. I was at an obnoxious little dinner party the other evening, talking about world affairs when this fellow said suddenly, "Let's run Groucho Marx for Vice-President." Naturally, I was touched. I asked why I should be singled out for this honor. Why should my friends want me to be Vice-President?

"Because," snarled my sponsor, "the Vice-President generally keeps his mouth shut. It might be an interesting experience for you."

So you can see that the boom didn't get a good start,

which is just as well, since, as I say, I am not a candidate for any office. But don't get me wrong. This isn't false modesty. If somebody wants to start another boom, the Vice-Presidency is right up my alley, although I'll admit it might take a little time before I could get used to listening to the Senate every day.

I remember that about forty years ago a vice-president made himself famous merely by announcing that what this country needed was a good five-cent cigar. What this country really needs is a good five-cent nickel. And barring that, a good five per cent income tax.

As a matter of fact, I've been making a few notes about what the country needs and, regardless of politics, here they are:

For one thing, the nation needs a good ham sandwich. I refer to the simple, old-fashioned (now obsolete) single-decker ham sandwich which was a national institution until the druggist, with his passion for mixing things, ruined it for us. As an experiment, I went into a drugstore yesterday and ordered a ham sandwich.

"Ham with what?" the clerk asked.

"Coffee," I told him.

"I mean," he said, "do you want the ham-and-tuna combination, the ham-sardine-and-tomato, or ham-bacon-and-broccoli? And will you have cole slaw or potato salad?"

"Just ham," I pleaded. "A plain ham sandwich, without even tomato or lettuce."

The young man looked bewildered, then went over to the drug counter to consult with the pharmacist, who was busy at the moment, making up a batch of Seconal pills for his customers who had been wiped out again in the market. He glowered at me suspiciously until I fled. That's the sort of thing this country is up against.

Another of our direst needs is a coat for carrying tobacco without making it necessary to carry a bulky, bulging pouch. It has been suggested that tailors make suits out of tobacco so that if you want to fill your favorite pipe, you would merely have to tear off a piece of the material and plug it into the bowl.

This is unsound on the face of it, because a suit with its lapels smoked off would be highly impractical. Where would you wear your campaign button or elk's tooth?

My suggestion is that only the vest be made of tobacco, because the vest is an otherwise useless garment. It isn't ornamental and it doesn't give much warmth. I believe that a nice, mild Burley-cut vest, trimmed with Turkish, would add a great deal to the comfort of the American male.

In designing this outfit, some enterprising tailor could also supply another need—a pair of pants that would automatically hide at night so that your wife couldn't possibly know where you were caching your bankroll. Making your pants vanish may sound a trifle visionary, but I have been making quite a bit of progress with the idea. I've already succeeded in making my shirt disappear, merely by sitting down at the bridge table with my wife.

I know a fellow who bid two hearts with only three quick tricks in his hand, and his wife disappeared. That, of course, solved his problem. He could then hang his pants out in the open at night. But this solution is not to be recommended generally, because I believe that wives have a definite place in the home. They're invaluable as mothers, and also for keeping you informed as to when the lady next door gets a new car, a new fur stole, or is taken out dancing. Wives are people who feel that they don't dance enough. Give them their way and you won't have to hide your pants at night because there will be nothing in them to conceal.

Another national need is laundries that will send you a sheet of pins with every shirt instead of making you pick the pins, one at a time, out of the collar or (if you don't spot them in time) your neck. My own laundryman and I have an understanding. Every time he sticks me with a pin I stick him with a bad check. His cries of anguish can be heard from Culver City to my bank in Beverly Hills.

We need, too, a vacuum cleaner that won't scare the daylights out of you by whining like a B-707 jet when you try to snatch a brief four-hour afternoon nap. At considerable expense and bother I've solved the problem in my own home, but, as you'll readily see, it's far from the ideal solution. I've placed land mines around my bedroom door. (Neutrals, of course, have been warned.) Thus, if the cleaner zooms within twenty feet of my room, it'll be a good joke on our maid. The only disadvantage is that, after a direct hit, you have to get a new vacuum cleaner. Also a new maid. And the mess on the floor is, of course, considerable.

Well, the list goes on and on—as long as Sonny Liston's arm. But before I get boomed into the Vice-Presidency and forced to bridle my unbridled tongue, there are a few more thoughtful little essays I must get out of my system. Which reminds me, what this country probably needs most of all is few thoughtful essayists.

2

On Thrift

The people who talk about the dear departed days are usually over fifty. They nostalgically remember the horse and buggy, the bicycle built for two, penny candy, and that structure in the back yard that looked like a telephone booth but wasn't. Many other cherished things have disappeared, but why go on? If you're over fifty you probably remember them as clearly as I do.

The word "thrifty," for example, has no meaning today except as a name for a chain of drug stores. The *Wall Street Journal* says that the entire country is living on a precarious precipice of debt; the government is deeply in hock and so are most of its citizens. It's a joy ride, they add, but nobody in Washington seems to give a damn.

In the old days, when people were poor they lived poor. Today they live rich. I've discussed this with many wage earners in the eight-to-ten-thousand-dollar-a-year class and, in most cases, they admit that almost everything they own, they don't—their automobiles, their television sets, their houses, and the furniture. Their philosophy seems to be, "What the hell—we may be dead tomorrow!" However, if their prediction is a few decades off, many of them will spend their old age living off the state.

Cleanliness may be next to godliness, but to my mind thriftiness would be closer. I consider myself one of the last survivors of a dying era. I'm the type that turns out the lights when I leave a room. I turn the water taps securely to make sure they don't drip. Although I have a cook, I go to the supermarket myself and pick out the food that she will eventually ruin. People are astonished when they see me at the vegetable bin, carefully weighing the merits of two heads of cabbage, pinching tomatoes, and an occasional tootsie. Since my face is fairly well known, this is frequently a source of embarrassment, but I can't help myself. I'm convinced that thrift, in my case, is an innate trait that springs from a debt-ridden childhood and can no more be overcome than old age (which I passed some years ago).

I am not alone in this. I have many prosperous friends who are also frugal in peculiar ways. I have a friend who uses a fresh handkerchief each day, but on retiring, before throwing the used one in the laundry hamper, he gives it one last stentorian blow. I questioned him about this one day and he said, "I try to get as much mileage as I can out of each day's handkerchief, and I don't feel too bad when I catch a cold. That's when I really get my money's worth!"

I have another friend (you didn't imagine I had two, did you?), who earns about two hundred thousand dollars a year. He will take you to Romanoff's in a Rolls Royce and then park it two or three blocks away so that he won't have to tip the parking attendant. It isn't that he's stingy. He explains, "If I go to an expensive restaurant and spend fifty or sixty dollars for dinner, I want the management to park my car gratis."

I know another chap who is completely bald, and yet whenever he goes to a restaurant, even in the winter, he leaves his hat in the car. As a result, he frequently has a heavy cold, and about twice a year he comes down with pneumonia. But he says he doesn't care. "I refuse to tip some hat check girl fifty cents just to hang my hat on a hook. I wouldn't mind so much if she kept the money, but she

doesn't get a penny of it. Part of the swag is kept by the restaurant and the rest goes to some sinister combine in Chicago that controls these concessions."

I give my wife a liberal allowance, but when we dine out I groan in despair when she suddenly discovers that she has no cigarettes. I then have to plank down a buck to some short-skirted babe for a pack of cigarettes that I can buy almost anywhere for two bits. Seventy-five cents shot! Almost the price of a Martini, which I desperately need after paying a dollar for a pack of cigarettes.

Jack Benny, in real life, is an extremely generous fellow, but his theatrical image is that of a parsimonious skinflint who would risk his life for a buck. People roar with laughter at his miserliness. They think it's terribly funny that he regards money as something that shouldn't be squandered. We'll see who laughs last!

Fred Allen, a great man (and, boy, could we use him today!), one summer rented a cottage in Maine for three hundred dollars for the season. Being an actor, and the landlord being from Maine, he was obliged to pay the rent in advance. Early in June Fred was offered two thousand dollars a week to write a short column every other day for one of the syndicates. This was long ago when two thousand dollars was still a lot of money, but Fred turned down the offer. I asked him why. "I paid three hundred dollars for that cottage up in Maine," he said, "and if I accept this job I'll have to stay in New York. I'd be out the three hundred dollars."

The syndicate then raised its offer to three thousand dollars a week. Again Fred turned it down. They then offered four thousand dollars and once more he refused.

"Why don't you forget about the three hundred dollars?" I asked. "You could take one week's salary from the syndicate and own that cottage outright."

But Allen, too, had curious notions about money. He was extremely generous but he couldn't stand waste. He was also extremely stubborn. "I paid three hundred dollars to live in that cottage this summer," he said, "and that landlord is not going to get my money for nothing!"

I once played a season on the Orpheum Circuit with a very funny comedian named Doc Rockwell. He had his own way of saving money. The first week in Chicago, Doc bought six blue serge double-breasted suits for one hundred and fifty dollars, and if you're any good at mathematics you know this comes to twenty-five dollars apiece. He would wear each suit for about a month and then, when it was partially covered with spots and a few rips, he would throw it away. He had it all figured out. "This way," he explained, "I don't have to pay for any cleaning and pressing and, besides, I'm always wearing a brand-new suit."

Years ago, when playing the small time, most actors used to dine at the Automat. The food was wonderful and I'm sure it still is but, unfortunately, I can't eat there any more because of the autograph hunters. For years I've been telling my daughter, Melinda, what wonderful restaurants they are. I told her that all you had to do was get a lot of nickels from the cashier, drop them in various slots and, presto, you had a meal fit for a king (assuming there are any still around).

The last time I went to New York I took Melinda along. We were on our way to a very expensive restaurant when she asked me if we couldn't have lunch at the Automat. I said, "No, you wouldn't like it. It's terribly crowded and the food isn't any good."

"But Daddy," she said, "you told me just a few weeks ago that the food is as good as at any restaurant in New York."

Well, she had me there. The pressure a child can put on a parent is beyond belief—unless you are a parent. So before I knew it I was standing in front of the cashier's cage at Horn and Hardart's Automat, changing enough nickels for two meals.

Melinda, far more excited than she would have been at "21" or the Pavillon, ran around dropping nickels into slots as though this was to be her last meal. I decided on a roast beef sandwich and carefully inserted ten nickels in the proper slot, but for some reason the little glass door didn't open. I then tapped gently on the window with a coin, but the door still didn't budge. I tried hammering on the door with my fist. Suddenly a stout woman came rushing out from behind the façade of glass windows and said, "Are you the gent who's been thumpin' on my window?"

"I certainly am," I answered.

"Well, don't y'know ya have to put in ten nickels t'get a fifty cent roast beef san'wich? Whatsamatter? You stupid 'r somethin'? Didn't ya go to school?"

By this time some of the other diners, overhearing the argument, began gathering around us and, to my dismay, recognized me. I tried to ignore them and again asked for my sandwich.

The female bruiser said, "Let me tell ya a thing 'r two. We get guys like you every day. Ya think, just because this is a automatic rest'rant, y'can get away with somethin'!"

By this time a goodly crowd surrounded us. A bus boy broke through and spotted me. "Hey," he said, "ain't you a big star on TV? What're ya arguin' with the poor dame for over a lousy nickel? Inna first place, what're ya eatin' in a dump like this for? If I had yer dough ya wouldn't catch me eatin' in no joint like this!"

I said, with considerable dignity, "I came here because my daughter wanted to eat at the Automat."

"Oh yeah?" he sneered. "So where's yer daughter?"

"Over there some place," I said. What I didn't know was that Melinda, not wishing to be embarrassed, had quietly sneaked out when the ruckus started and was waiting for me outside. I imagine she expected me to come out soon, on my head.

The argument with the bus boy and the female wrestler continued. And now, to make everything still sillier, people began asking for my autograph. A heavy-set woman behind me, determined to attract my attention, was jerking my coat-tails. Lucky for me she wasn't tugging at my trousers; otherwise I would soon have been standing there in my jockey shorts.

The floorwalker (or whoever he was, manager perhaps) came over and said, "Mr. Marx, I've always enjoyed your work, but why are you making such a scene over a nickel? You should be ashamed of yourself."

"Why?" I asked indignantly. "Just because I want my roast beef sandwich?"

"You know our machines don't lie," he said. "If you dropped ten nickels into the roast beef sandwich slot you would now be enjoying as fine a sandwich as you can get any place in New York."

The woman from behind the glass windows chimed in, "He only put in nine nickels and he knows y'need ten for a roast beef san'wich! Why don't he stick in another nickel an' get his lousy san'wich?"

The manager turned on her accusingly, "Did I hear you call our sandwich a *lousy* sandwich?!"

"Oh no, sir, I didn't mean our san'wich was lousy," she explained hurriedly. "I only meant he was a lousy cheap-skate for not puttin' in the extra lousy nickel."

Between the back-and-forth dialogue and the scribbling of autographs and worrying whether, by this time, Melinda had been picked up by white slavers and was now on a ship bound for Brazil, I was ready to beat a retreat.

"It's not the nickel, it's the principle of the thing," I said. "Just give me back my ten nickels and I'll dine in some bistro where I'm treated with the respect that a star is entitled to!"

The woman poured nine nickels into my chubby fist. I threw them up in the air and said, "There! That'll show you that money means nothing to me!"

I then stalked out, picked up Melinda and went to the Colony, where we had a lovely lunch for $27.60. And I want to announce to the whole world that I will never set foot in the Automat again until they have the decency to send me the nickel they still owe me.

3

On Luck

 No one can be successful without luck. One could have the brain of Einstein, the shrewdness of Barney Baruch, and the wisdom of Thoreau, but without Lady Luck in your corner you might just as well stay in your room and turn on the gas.

I didn't just ad lib this last statement. It was uttered by Schopenhauer one day while he was hunting wild boar in the Black Forest. As far as I know, there isn't a word of truth in the sentence I just dashed off (I mean about Schopenhauer) but I feel pretty safe making this statement. With that nut in Russia polluting the air with all kinds of fancy fallout, no one has time to check the veracity of any statement made by anyone about anything. And now that we've got this disjointed introduction out of the way, let's talk about luck and the part it plays in success.

If, in addition to luck, you happen to have talent, well, kid, you've got it made! The world will beat a path to your doorstep to buy your mousetrap or whatever it is you happen to be selling. It was phrased concisely some years ago by William Shakespeare when he wrote, "There is a tide in the affairs of men which, taken at the flood, leads on to fortune." It reduces itself to this. You have to be in the right place at the right time, but when it comes, you'd better have something on the ball.

During the rich, early days of Hollywood when the five major studios produced almost all the movies that were shown around the world, the big earners used to toss their money around as though they printed it themselves. Everybody who was anybody played polo. With few exceptions they didn't play well, but they enjoyed falling off their horses, and if one of the players broke a leg, they shot him.

The head of one of these studios was so wild about the game that he rarely walked around without a polo mallet tucked under his arm. Frequently, during a story conference, he would order one of his cheaper writers to get down on his hands and knees and then ride him around the office, just to keep in trim. This scribe wasn't crazy about doubling for a horse, but he didn't have much choice in the matter. He needed the job. He was a lousy writer and, besides, he owed back alimony to three earlier wives.

Then came the high income tax. As the rates got higher the horses got fewer. Many of the boys who had strings of polo ponies began selling them to South American dictators. The few nags that were left were eaten at barbecues. Incidentally, until you've tasted barbecued leg of polo pony, you haven't lived! Polo ceased to be the social barometer and the stars began looking around for cheaper ways to impress one another.

Then someone discovered tennis. Here was a sport almost

anyone could play and afford. All you needed was a sweat band, some sweat, a pair of sneakers, white flannels, some racquets, and, oh yes, a tennis court.

Some of the boys became pretty good at the game. One chap I knew (by name, Theodore Flunk), eager to be the town's top player, ripped out all his orange and lemon trees and even his kumquats, and had a professional tennis court installed in his back yard. He was a bachelor and lived alone in a very pretty house which was neatly tended and kept in order by a Japanese houseboy.

Mr. Flunk made it a practice to play a set or two in the morning before going to the studio. He was confident that if he became a topflight player, he had a good chance of being appointed head of a studio.

It wasn't always easy for him to get an opponent, and without one he had no one to hit the ball to or worse yet, to return the ball after he'd smacked it. Desperate, he asked the houseboy if he would like to hit the ball around with him. The boy gave a large, toothy smile, bowed low, and said he would be extremely honored to help his worthy master to perfect his game.

Surprisingly enough, the boy played a fairly good game, not good enough to beat his boss but good enough to make it an interesting contest. His employer usually won 6–2 or 6–1. Occasionally, if he'd had a tough time wrestling with some reluctant tootsie the night before, he would win 6–3, 6–4.

One afternoon Mr. Flunk returned home unexpectedly, just in time to see his houseboy tucking three bottles of expensive Scotch into a fiber suitcase. He was angry. This was a hell of a way to betray his confidence. He had paid the boy a generous salary, had given him comfortable living quarters, and all the food he could eat on the premises. Obviously there was no point in being a bachelor if his houseman was going to filch his booze. If he was going to get robbed, he might just as well get married.

So, in cold, measured tones, he informed his Oriental crook and houseman that two weeks from that date he was through. He pointed out that he wasn't really angry, just terribly, terribly hurt. He told this misbegotten son of the Far East that the swiping of three quarts of his best Scotch had shaken his faith in the young man and, therefore, he thought it best for him to pack his kimono and tennis sneakers and clear out.

However, he still wanted his tennis game, so the next morning they went out to the court as usual. In approximately twelve minutes the houseboy polished off Mr. Flunk 6–0, 6–0. If you are a tennis buff, you know this is as decisive a score as you can lose by.

The first day Mr. Flunk attributed his ignominious defeat to sheer bad luck. The second day, with another 6–0, 6–0 defeat for his pains, he attributed his loss to the starlet he'd been out with the previous night. The third day, having lost by the same score as on the first two days, he began to suspect that perhaps some agency other than Dame Fortune had a hand in this business.

Well, there's little point in going on. They played daily for two weeks. In those fourteen days the boss didn't win a single game.

Just before his servant departed, his ex-employer grilled him. "How come I used to beat you every day, but in the last two weeks I haven't been able to win a single set? Not even a game!"

"Well, sir," the boy grinned, exposing two rows of large even teeth, "while I was in your employ I did everything I could to please you. That is the Oriental way. I knew that if I lost, it made you happy. So I lost. It wasn't always easy. Then, sir, after you discharged me, I had no more reason to let you win."

"That may be true," admitted the crestfallen Mr. Flunk, "but I'm supposed to be a pretty good tennis player. How is it you were able to beat me so handily?"

"Ah, so," the boy bowed low. "Sir," he said, "I wasn't always a houseboy. Not so long ago I came over here from Japan and I played tennis every day, all over America. You see, sir, I was then captain of the Japanese International Tennis Team."

4

On Talent

 Some years ago a Ziegfeld show opened in Boston. It was an historic opening, but then all of Ziegfeld's opening nights were something to conjure with, as Mr. Jessel would put it.

Once you've said Ziegfeld, you've said everything! He had the most beautiful girls, the most glamorous scenery, and the funniest comics.

I won't tell the name of the female star, but in a musical where even the stage hands were picked for their beauty, this girl stood out as one of the great dreamboats of the theater. She didn't have too much talent but she sang fairly well and danced about as gracefully as most of the show girls, which wasn't saying much.

Unfortunately, I didn't know her too well, and if I had, it wouldn't have done me any good, for she liked to drink and I didn't. Besides, she was being kept by a Brazilian plantation owner. She wasn't an alcoholic but she liked three or four hearty nips before and during the performance.

In the first act the curtain rose on a rustic scene. The stage was banked with roses and our little girl was seated in a floral swing festooned with enough flowers to bury the whole front row. As this seductive bit of femininity swung out over the audience, she trilled a lyric so banal that I'm convinced she must have written it herself. "Swing me high, swing me low, swing me over the garden wall."

But nobody cared what she sang. They didn't even listen to her. They just looked. There was hardly a husband in the audience who wasn't hypnotized by her beauty, and there was hardly a wife who wasn't glaring at her husband.

During the preceding two weeks in Philadelphia, she had sung a verse and chorus of this song to perfunctory applause. But on opening night in Boston a strange magic seemed to fill the theater and the applause was deafening. Again and again the curtain had to be raised. Through eight choruses she swung her pretty legs out over the audience.

The cast, standing in the wings, was mystified by this unusual ovation. The stage hands were puzzled. Ziegfeld was astonished. I doubt if the walls of any theater had ever echoed to a wilder demonstration.

What had she added to that little song that had led this evening's audience virtually to riot?

The fact of the matter is, she hadn't added anything. She had merely subtracted something. This memorable night she had taken more than her customary few nips and, bleary with booze, she had neglected to don her panties.

The moral of this little tale is threefold: if you have talent, sooner or later it will out; it doesn't pay to hide your light under a bushel; and if you don't get the right answer by simple addition, reverse your field—try subtraction.

5

On Polygamy (and How to Attain It)

In many ways governments resemble people. They, too, make mistakes, some of them beauts. One of the greatest bloomers of the last century occurred when the United States government notified the Mormons that polygamy would have to stop—or else.

If you happen to be a student of early Americana, which I doubt you are, or you wouldn't be frittering away your time reading this bilge, you would know that originally there was a practical reason why the Mormons practiced polygamy. The men were considerably outnumbered, and to be sure there would be enough children to go around, a husband was not only permitted, but urged, to have an indefinite number of wives.

Unfortunately, I wasn't lucky enough to be there at the time, and so my knowledge of this era is meager; but I never read anywhere that the Mormon women were dissatisfied.

191

I regret to say that this plural wife custom is now disappearing in other lands. Some countries had harems, others, concubines. In some countries the men just dropped all the euphemisms and simply swapped trollops, hoping with each swap to improve on what they had.

What I'm driving at is that the male in most countries still practices a modified form of polygamy, only the name has been changed. In France, for example, it is not unusual for a husband to have a wife and a mistress. However, if in addition to these two he's also having a fling with a fringe tootsie, both the wife and the mistress are outraged and the combination lover, husband, and cheat may well wind up with a large French bread knife between his ribs.

In Latin countries, where the Church is dominant, it is virtually impossible to obtain a divorce. I don't know how the male circumvents this, but his extracurricular activities

seem to be in no way diminished by the pressures he has to contend with. No dictum can discourage a normal, red-blooded male from gazing lustfully at any young piece of baggage that wiggles by. I realize that this is no earthshaking, original observation, but it's something all men understand and most women are reluctant to believe or accept.

I am not prepared to say that all American husbands are untrue to their wives. *Au contraire*, I think most husbands are faithful in their fashion. Horace says, with an assist from Ernest Dowson, "I have been faithful to thee, Cynara, in my fashion." This is a pretty qualified statement, and Horace should be ashamed of himself.

I merely quoted Horace to let you know that, though I am but a lowly vaudeville actor who has squandered his best years touring through some of the crummiest burgs in America, I too, out of sheer desperation and boredom, have skimmed the classics. And you, dear reader, may discover that even a beggar who has worshiped (though half-heartedly) at the feet of learning, may have something to offer you besides the mundane study of sex and its ramifications. And please forgive me for calling sex mundane. Mundane, indeed! What a word to describe this glorious experience that Mother Nature has improvised to keep us all on our toes and occasionally on our back.

However, whether because of fear, social ostracism, the penalties of alimony, or the desire to keep the family under one roof, the average male sternly represses his basic and normal yearnings.

In my time, I'm sure I've read seven or eight million words describing the cravings of the average man for a woman other than his wife. Curiously enough, I've rarely read an article where the female yearns for someone other than her husband.

It seldom occurs to the average married man (who is basically a stupe) with a receding hairline, bifocals, and a middle-aged paunch, that perhaps his little woman, bless her, may also get a thrill, if only a vicarious one, watching Rock Hudson or Tony Curtis plant a long, endearing, lipstick-smearing smack on the lovely creature he will eventually seduce. Isn't it conceivable that, while she sits there in that gilded movie palace, munching popcorn and scraping dead chewing gum off her left shoe with her right foot, she, too, would like to be in Rock's or Tony's arms, replacing that pallid ingénue he is trying publicly to rape by innuendo?

Picture the average household in the gray, dim morning as the husband leaves for work. Before departing he hurriedly tosses his wife a badly-aimed kiss which invariably lands on her left ear. This is hardly a replacement for the soul-kiss he used to bestow on her when courting her in the back seat of his six-year-old Buick. You see, hubby is in a bit of a bind. He is rushing to the office to try to persuade the nymphomaniac who takes his dictation (and is officially known as his secretary) that unless she is willing to swallow the oral contraceptives he has surreptitiously purchased for her from his friendly neighborhood druggist, both he and she will be bounced from the organization or establishment, and may have to spend the rest of their years together subsisting on the miserable pittance the government doles out to those who are unemployed.

Meanwhile, back at the ranch, isn't it possible that the little woman, too, particularly after watching three hours of Rock and Tony crushing theoretical virgins to their bosoms, might crave someone younger and newer than her husband? Someone with a flat stomach and some hair? (And I don't mean on his stomach, I mean on his skull.)

While he is fiddling around the office, has it ever occurred to him that his wife, especially if the children are off to school or away at college, also has her temptations throughout the day? She, too, has red corpuscles flowing through her veins. She, too, would once again like to experience the thrill of a pair of muscular, hairy arms encircling her bosom. She, too, is no longer titillated by the casual good-by peck in the morning and the reappearance of her indifferent sluggard in the evening, returning from a pregnant day at the office. There are the butcher, the baker, the mailman, the milkman, and the television repair man. (This last character, if my house is any criterion, probably spends more

time in her living room than he does in his own.) Some of these men are young, handsome, and available. Their costumes may not be as glamorous as Rock's or Tony's, their locks may not be as carefully curled, their speech may not be as romantic, but underneath their workaday exteriors they, too, are men, with the same passions and desires as those of the most expensive movie heroes.

"The lover's pleasure, like that of the hunter, unfortunately lies in the chase, and the brightest beauty loses half its charm, as the flower its perfume, when the eager hand can reach it too easily. There must be doubt: there must be difficulty and danger." (Sir Walter Scott.)

Sir Walter, I thank you. That's as classy a piece of writing as I've encountered in many a day, and I'm glad you're in the public domain so that I don't have to pay some thieving publisher for filching this observation. You have said in six lines, what I have been trying, in my own lumbering way, to explain in six pages.

It is evident that the normal male hasn't changed much since Sir Walter wrote those deathless words. He's still no good. He still has all the morals of the most promiscuous mixed-breed mongrel.

I hope you realize that what I have written about wives is mostly conjecture and therefore not to be taken too seriously. My guess is that she is fairly content with her own little world, the children's tonsils, the report card from school, an occasional movie, a bridge or gin rummy game, and her husband, the lout, who, as I write these words, lies spread out on the couch, snoring loud enough to drown out even the Bullwinkle cartoon show.

And what about that thing that lies there sprawling, his brutish mouth wide open, his arms dangling from their sockets? Occasionally he emits a loud grunt, which is his conception of togetherness. If you are an animal lover I'm sure you know that a dog, when sleeping, will frequently whine querulously and shudder convulsively, which means he's dreaming longingly of those good old days when he was a wolf and was hot on the chase. And this, my friends, is precisely what the alleged head of the house is dreaming about.

Man will never learn. When first he meets the girl of his dreams, it may be on a Sunday morning in church, it may be at a tennis match, or it may be at the restaurant where he daily gulps the business man's luncheon (with dessert, 25¢ extra). Girls, it has been said, are everywhere, so it could be almost anywhere that the male is stung by the love bug.

What attracted him to her? Her eyes? Her legs? Was it something mysteriously feminine about her that no other girl seemed to possess? She is young, cute, and romantic and her speech is fairly intelligent. As they get to know each other more intimately (I mean in a nice way, of course), they both discover that they are ecstatically happy when together and miserable when apart. And then, oh happy day, if she is smart enough not to spring her mother on him too unexpectedly, they will get married.

No matter how many married couples they know, some unhappy, some happy, it seems inconceivable that anything could ever mar the joy they presently find in each other. I am sure that if they ever had any doubts or misgivings about their future happiness, neither wild horses nor her father could drag them to the altar.

It is well known that young love is a temporary form of insanity and that the only cure for it is instant marriage.

What these pathetic innocents don't know is that the stresses and strains of matrimony don't appear until they have gone through what, in the navy, is termed a "shakedown cruise."

When one considers the pitfalls and traps that await them it seems to me incredible that so many couples remain married. There are so many obstacles to overcome; the intrusion of the children at the wrong moment, the intrusion of the children at any moment, the breakdown of the garbage disposal, and money. Don't ever underestimate the importance of money. I know it's often been said that money won't make you happy and this is undeniably true, but everything else being equal, it's a lovely thing to have around the house.

As a marriage grows older, sex eventually recedes to its proper proportions. Oh, you think not? Well, let's say it's not as important as it was those first three wonderful days in Niagara Falls or that weekend in a San Antonio motel. But my guess is that, in the average home five years after the marriage takes place, there is more bickering and acrimonious debate over money than any other subject.

A well-known doctor, one of my more cynical friends, once told me that one of *his* more cynical friends (a well-known philanderer from Mittel Europa) boasted that he had a very happy marriage and attributed this entirely to the fact that he constantly practiced adultery. In his quaint Viennese patois, the doctor's friend explained, "Although I love my wife, marriage to me is a business arrangement. Whenever I am untrue to her, naturally, I feel guilty. Whenever I feel guilty I salve my conscience by buying her some magnificent gift; perhaps a piece of jewelry, perhaps a down payment on a foreign car, occasionally a new fur coat. If I don't feel too guilty, my conscience will sometimes permit me to settle for five pounds of very expensive caviar. I'm convinced she doesn't know of my indiscretions," he went on, "but even if she did, isn't she better off than the average wife whose husband is faithful but never gives her anything?"

Perhaps this is an isolated case. The average husband cannot afford to assuage his guilt with bribery, which is virtually what it amounts to. This is a device in which only the extremely wealthy can indulge.

I'll conclude this with a quote from Lord Chesterfield who, for years, has manufactured one of the finest cigarettes in America and, though he's been tempted many times, has never stooped to turning out filtered cigarettes. He said, and I quote, "There are two objects in marriage: love or money. If you marry for love you will certainly have some very happy days; if for money, you will have no happy days and probably no uneasy ones."

In my time I've read clearer statements, but you must remember that Lord Chesterfield is in the business of hawking cigarettes and his thinking apparatus has undoubtedly been befuddled by his own smoke.

6

On (and off) Bodies

Each year I read optimistic and enthusiastic articles describing the new automobiles that will appear next season. It is predicted they will have engines in the rear, seats made out of formaldehyde, bodies made out of molybdenum, and steering wheels made out of French pastry. (In case you get hungry on a long trip.)

If those boys in Detroit can turn out a new car every year, why can't someone manufacture a new man? If there ever was a contraption that needed improving, it's the human body. If this current model is old Mother Nature's masterpiece, obviously the old girl is a little on the jerky side and needs a few years at a good engineering school.

Let us begin at the bottom and work our way up. Here we find the feet. Feet are utterly without beauty. Would any man reading this go out with a girl who resembled his feet? Of course not. They are usually gnarled and misshapen

201

from being whacked against furniture and high curbs, and they constantly need new shoes, socks, arch supports, adhesive tape and nail clippers.

Now come with me for a moment into the world of fantasy. Let us suppose your feet grew in the shape of wheels. Wouldn't this be the scientific breakthrough of the century? You could roll around and see your friends, you could roll to the supermarket, and in the evening when you came home from work your wife could tie a suction bag around your neck and use you for a vacuum cleaner. (When she isn't using you for a doormat.)

Now, my friends, move up twenty-four inches and what do we encounter? A flabby thigh. Then move down a few inches and what do we see? That's right, the knee. No one has ever been able to figure out what purpose the knee serves. It toils not, neither does it shin. (This is known as a literary pun and is always greeted with about five minutes of deadly silence, after which the publisher, if he is any sort of an editor, will give the author a murderous kick in the shins.) The knee is hardly worth discussing. Functionally, it's a disgrace. It is constantly getting out of joint and requires almost as much attention as a second-hand lawn mower. It is true that in the old days the knee played an important part in love-making. A lover would slide off the parlor sofa and plop down on one knee when declaring his affection to the girl of his dreams. The invention of the gasoline motor, however, gradually changed all of this. The back seat of an automobile at the local drive-in movie proved itself a much more practical setting and, in a few short years, the parlor sofa deteriorated into a useless and moth-eaten antique and the girl of his dreams now had four children. (It was a very long movie.)

The stomach, or belly, is a prominent part of the human body, particularly if you lap up a lot of beer. But I am sure a smart designer could have rigged it up more efficiently. The stomach serves two purposes. It holds your dinner and, what is much more important, it allegedly holds up your trousers. Unfortunately, we have to breathe, which means that whenever we inhale the trousers drop from two to four inches, leaving the pants at half-mast. This could easily have been avoided had the hip bone been extended six inches on each side. The trousers would then hang naturally without the aid of belt or suspenders, and the rear of a man's pants

wouldn't sag as though it were filled with three or four frying pans.

The less said about the arms, the better. They grow out of nothing, they swing aimlessly back and forth, and they give the wearer a grotesque and unfinished appearance. Even the ugly baboon, supposedly several notches lower than man in the social scale, is better equipped. A full-grown baboon's arms are long enough to reach the ground without stooping over, which enables him to pluck bananas while strolling down the street, not to mention picking up cigar butts and small coins out of the gutter, with no loss of dignity.

The neck is a short drain pipe that rises up out of the shoulders and disappears into the bottom of the head. It is usually decorated with an Adam's apple and an untidy collar. The Adam's apple is a medium-sized meat ball that keeps running up and down the front of the neck looking helplessly for its mate. It is an unfortunate monstrosity that nature, angry at her handiwork, has left on our doorstep and there is nothing we can do about it. Many people attempt to hide it by wrapping a necktie around it, but in most cases the necktie is even uglier than the apple.

The neck would be much more useful if it were equipped with ball bearings. This would enable the head to swing completely around on its axis and, if necessary, eventually return to its original position. Equipped with a revolving head, a man could walk down the street and, if he noticed a choice number strolling past in the opposite direction, he could quickly swing his head toward her and speculate upon whether that's the way he would like to spend the afternoon. By spinning the head occasionally in the other direction, he would also reduce the danger of bumping into strange pedestrians and, perhaps, his wife.

This brings us to the teeth, the sentinels of the mouth. The average man spends fifty per cent of his salary on his

family, twenty-five per cent on tootsies, and twenty-five per cent on his choppers. Let us look into the mouth of a man who has just celebrated his fiftieth birthday. What do you see? In addition to a small piece of birthday cake, you will note a miscellaneous collection of inlays, concrete fillings, porcelain jackets, and a coated tongue. In fact, you will find practically everything but teeth. But should the teeth be blamed for this? Of course not! The teeth are innocent bystanders. They didn't ask to be a part of the mouth. Had we been built scientifically there wouldn't be any mouth at all. You naturally ask, "How would we eat?" Frankly, I don't know, but I'll give it some thought over the week end.

We now come to man's crowning glory—the hair. The top of the head is apparently the only spot where hair cannot be grown with any consistent degree of success. In most cases, all the scalp acquires is a smooth, slippery surface as bleak as Death Valley. Perhaps scientific agriculture can solve this problem. Farmers, when they were not too busy in Washington demanding ever more subsidies for their wheat or succotash, long ago discovered that their soil deteriorated unless they rotated their crops. For example, if one year they raised corn, the following year they raised wheat or cabbage or, in desperate cases, even eggplant.

Now isn't it reasonable to believe that the scalp might respond to similar treatment? In the winter we would grow hair on our heads, and then in the spring, as the hair began thinning and falling into the soup, the scalp could be plowed up and string beans planted. I particularly recommend string beans, for they are green and curly, they grow to a good height and require very little attention. Around October, they could be clipped and made into a nice salad. The next year the same thing could be done with cabbage. A man could have a head of hair in the winter and a head of cabbage in the summer. (This same joke can also be used for a head of lettuce, but there's no point in whipping a dead head.)

I could go on endlessly pointing out the hideous mistakes that nature has made, but my time is short and if my readers will examine one another carefully and honestly, I am sure they'll be willing to admit that everything I've said about the human body has been, if anything, an understatement.

EPILOGUE
OFF MY ROCKER

A thin, wrinkled wisp of a man can be observed dimly in the darkness, rocking ceaselessly to and fro in a pre-Kennedy antique chair. It is our onetime Mangy Lover. He puffs slowly on a deep-colored meerschaum. The light in the fireplace grows dim. The tiny fire is banked with faintly glowing coals that match the passions that once burned so brightly in our Lothario's heart.

A faint smile plays around his lips as he thinks once again of his many conquests; of the international beauties who capitulated before his flashing eyes and jaunty figure. The lucky ones who could not say him nay dance gaily past in his memories. The unhappy few who rejected him plod mournfully past, cursing the stupid fates that cheated them of the thrills that could have been theirs had they been bold enough to accept his challenge to swim in the seas of his passions. The smile grows wider as he thinks of those hair-breadth escapes from irate husbands and sex-crazed lovers.

Our hero has no regrets. All his life he has drunk deeply at the fountain of love and helped himself liberally and impartially to the luscious fruits that await only those who have

no fear of life but live alone for lust, contemptuous of the dangers that lurk inside a woman's arms.

Had he so desired he could have been a prince in a counting house, a commander in the armed forces, a Hamlet in the theater, but even as a callow youth he had been marked by an erotic destiny. He knew his life's work was to be the relentless pursuit of the elusive and tantalizing female.

Perhaps he, too, could be called a hunter; not of the brutish grizzly, not of the gargantuan bull elephant, and certainly not of the snarling lioness protecting her litter. The image of the hunter the world knows is a juvenile who has never grown up and never will. He is a boy who has never attained man's estate. He sets forth for the jungle armed with the standard paraphernalia of his ilk: the carbine, the machete, and the kinky-haired bushbeater. He is ready, at the drop of a pith helmet, to slaughter some innocent animal who has nothing with which to defend itself but a set of teeth and a few pitiful claws.

Is this the challenge for an adult male? Heavens, no! No more than the real challenge is to possess some woman by making her yours through the holy bonds of matrimony. We all know that there is hardly a female alive who can resist the hand offered in marriage by some dolt eager to work his fingers to the bone for her. Making love to your wife is like shooting at sitting ducks.

The connoisseur of sex, the true misogamist, scoffs at these easy avenues of love. What he wants he wants but for the moment. He sneers at the marriage ring that ties. True, he craves the pulsating body of the female, but it must be with no strings of platinum, no entangling alliances. Once she surrenders, he is off to ravage other fields.

With the gifts nature has hung upon him, he has no problems. Women are but putty in his hands; melting wax to the glow in his eyes. He brings them all down to size. This is the mark of the real hunter.

But why go on? It has been a long and wonderful charade. Though now he is but an ancient libertine, he has never lost his wisdom. He is fully aware of the sexual decay that age bestows impartially on the heroic and the cowardly. He is aware of his limitations. He realizes that the creaking he hears is not the sound of the rocker, but is just the noise of his withered carcass, groaning in despair. For all his so-called conquests, he knows his victories, though not entirely Pyrrhic, have taken their inevitable toll.

But now even the faint glow in the ashes has disappeared. The eyelids grow heavy and soon he sinks into a deep sleep.

No, dear reader, he is not dead. But as you and I know, he might as well be.

A NOTE ON THE AUTHOR
BY GROUCHO MARX

To write an autobiography of Groucho Marx would be as asinine as to read an autobiography of Groucho Marx. He can no more be put on paper than Lawrence of Arabia, garbed in his burnoose and turban, can be pulled out of the hot sands of the Middle East and set down in bald print.

Incredible as it may seem, these two had much in common. They both had a wide streak of the mystic. Lawrence, saturnine and moody, taciturn and reticent. Groucho, piercing of eye and ungainly of gait. Yet these two, in less time than it takes to tell, captured the imagination of millions of fanatical followers. Even the whining schoolboy with his morning face, creeping unwillingly to school, had heard and read about them.

I doubt if the foreseeable future, or even the ages, will see the end of the morbid and generally obscene speculation that grew up around these two heroic, historical figures.

This generation, above all, living as it does under the constant terror of world-wide obliteration, can nevertheless consider itself extremely lucky to have breathed the same air on the same globe that harbored these two legendary figures, so different and yet so much alike.

Lawrence of Arabia, streaking across the wide distances of the mysterious desert on his swift steed (no beggar on horseback, he), or leisurely jogging along on his two-humped camel, keeping an appointment with who knows what destiny . . . and, on the other side of the globe, Groucho the Inevitable, living precariously on the outskirts of limbo, bereft of steed or dromedary, transporting himself hither and yon by shank's mare, but yet indomitable of spirit, whistling gaily as he treads the boulevards, his smile roguish, his leer flirtatious and irresistible.

Groucho's most redeeming feature was that he, though generally as garrulous as the most sex-starved and frustrated virgin, could, when some fair maiden's honor was at stake, bridle his tongue so tightly that no man alive could shake it asunder. This, to the average married nymphomaniac, meant more than words can tell.

So, dear reader, though they lived worlds apart and though I am no seer, nor a prophet of any moment, I predict that some day these two will meet; perhaps on some other planet, perhaps on some mountain top, perhaps riding a monsoon on high over the skies of the Indian Ocean.

These are men to give one pause.